# TIME AND TIDE
## The Life of a Thames Waterman

JACK GASTER

AMBERLEY

First published 2010

Amberley Publishing Plc
Cirencester Road, Chalford,
Stroud, Gloucestershire, GL6 8PE
www.amberleybooks.com

British Library Cataloguing in Publication Data.
A catalogue record for this book is available from the British Library.

ISBN 978 1 84868 844 5

Typeset in 10pt on 12pt Sabon.
Typesetting and Origination by Fonthill.
Printed in the UK.

# CONTENTS

# FOREWORD

Jack Gaster had written several chapters of this book after request from the various organisations he had been involved with.

About twelve years ago he undertook the writing of the whole book, the effort of which very nearly killed him, as he had a series of strokes, causing major health problems.

His computer then broke and his son David's laptop was stolen, so all electronic versions of this book were lost.

Fortunately Jack had sent a paper copy to Waterman Hall which was found by Professor Alan Williams, who involved Amberley Publishing, to produce this book. They scanned the manuscript and David tidied it up, removing the vast majority of incorrect symbols from the words.

Jack also wrote the last two chapters of this book, now at the age of eighty-six.

It is hoped that the history of the Thames, and of those people associated with it will be as stimulating for you as it has been for those involved in creating this very unique book.

# CHAPTER ONE

# INDENTURED APPRENTICE

It was to some extent chance that brought me to Watermans Hall, on that second Tuesday in September 1937, where I was to be indentured as an Apprentice Waterman and Lighterman of the River Thames at just fourteen years old.

I suppose it had all begun at the age of four, when my favourite uncle went off to join the boy service in the Royal Navy. From that day on I wanted to be a sailor and my every spare moment was spent looking into books of the sea and ships, longing for the day when I would be old enough to start out on a life of great adventure, sailing the high seas.

As a youngster, I lived in the very heart of the Docklands – Burdett Road, Bow, London, E3, (situated at the back of the local fire station). Here, even the firemen had sailor-like hats, when they were not wearing their shiny brass helmets. I used to watch them for hours whilst they carried out their escape drills on the practice tower behind the building that housed their gleaming highly polished escape and pump engines.

Much to the worry and anxiety of my parents I was a roamer, and as I grew older I began to venture further afield, often finding myself down by some of the canals or the riverside. When there I would stay for hours, watching the activities of craft being moved by tugs, or barges laden with timber or coal, being pulled along the canals by the large horses straining on the tow-lines, each with an attendant handler who made sure that the line did not foul any obstruction along the waterway, never dreaming that someday I would be doing both the horse and the steers-mans job, along a number of the canals around London.

I undertook trips to the Tower of London during my school holidays (official or unofficial) as often as I could afford – a return, from Burdett Road Station to Fenchurch Street Station, on the old London and North Eastern Railway cost me a penny – from my limited pocket money and my Saturday earnings from the greengrocers (for washing or peeling the beetroot, and delivering the vegetables to the local Jewish fraternity who did not work on their Sabbath).

When arriving at the Tower, I would make my way to the river front above the Traitors Gate, looking out onto the tideway. Here I would sit astride some of the old cannons and mortars that had been won in some far-off sea battle and brought home as prizes by our victorious sailors, to be used in the many wars and battles fought by myself and fellow schoolboys on that wonderful playground, on Saturday afternoons or during school holidays. Of course all the ships that came through Tower Bridge were targets if they flew anything but a Red or White Ensign.

I even ventured as far away as Greenwich Park, walking down past the old West India Dock gates along West India Dock Road, then turning into West Ferry Road following the riverside road to where it crossed over the swing bridge which spanned the old Millwall Dock entrance – alas the entrance has not been in use since it was damaged back in 1941 by a bomb that destroyed the outer gates (the South West India Dock entrance could admit shipping for the Millwall Dock, so it was not considered worth the effort and cost of repair during the war years).

I then made my way along to the Island Gardens where a foot tunnel entered by a stairway, or a lift that descended into a shaft covered by a cupola, allowed pedestrians to walk under the river and then surface, by a similar stairway or lift shaft, on the south side of the Thames at Greenwich. It is still in use today, though the area where it surfaces, on the Greenwich side, has undergone a dramatic change. Whereas before, it was next to a waterfront Public House, a public causeway, and a drawdock, it now has the famous Cutty Sark and the Gypsy Moth for company.

If like me, you are interested in watching the London Marathon each year, you will appreciate how I cannot fail to retrace some of my boyhood ventures along London's riverside. Many of the old riverside wharves and warehouses have long gone, to be replaced by modern housing and office developments that have opened up wonderful views of the river that were denied to us by the high walls and gates that usually surrounded some of the older buildings.

Once on the south side of the river, a walk up through Greenwich Park to the Observatory made the journey worthwhile because it opened up a wonderful vista of Limehouse and Greenwich reaches; with the ships moored to the several wharves, jettyies and buoys in that area, and sailing barges tacking their way up or down stream, depending on the flow of the tide, to their respective destinations.

It was pure magic and I was captivated. Needless to say, once the wander bug got me I sought further afield, and soon found the Woolwich Ferry, though that required a tram journey when I could afford it. A penny went a long way in those days – for sixpence an all-day ticket would take you anywhere the tram lines reached. The ferry, however, was a bus ride or a very long walk from Canning Town or East Ham. Once there, I would spend hours on the ferry, crossing back and forth from the north to the south side of the river until the crew got a bit fed up with us (I always found more fellow travellers), then we would hop off and catch the next boat.

We would go down to the passenger deck where we could look at the engineers through the large viewing windows as they operated the polished steel levers that controlled the giant pistons that drove the enormous paddles on either side of the ferry. These could be glimpsed through the openings of the paddle boxes as they splashed through the water, rising to go full circle as they propelled the ferry from side to side leaving a foaming wake astern. Then we made our way up on deck to watch as the skipper rang down on the telegraph to indicate what movements he required of the giant paddles. The engineer would move the shiny steel levers to crank the paddles in a backward or forward movement to manoeuvre the vessels into the terminals on either side of the river, there to discharge the lorries and horse drawn carts that regularly plied the dock areas, together with the pedestrian traffic who preferred the free trip across the river rather than the walk through the foot tunnel, a distance of some half a mile. This had to be undertaken when the ferry was not running as in the case of dense fog or after the last boat at 11.30 p.m.

This was the London that I knew and loved as I was growing up. I did get terribly jealous when a school friend of mine, who lived alone with his mother, had the chance to go to a Nautical Training School. I pleaded with my father to let me go with him, and know now that dad had my best interest at heart, though at the time I was really upset. 'No my lad, your uncle Steve is going to take you as an Apprentice on the River when you are fourteen, so you have only a couple more years to wait. In the meantime get some swimming practice in, it is something you must be able to do.'

I suppose it was this advice that led me to a venture which got me into hot water in more ways than one. On one of my trips round dockland I found myself down by a draw dock next to Northumberland Wharf on the Isle of Dogs. It was a hot summer's day and the tide was in. Several youngsters were in swimming in the 'buff' so, not to be left out I joined them.

We were climbing on a green-painted wreck of a marking boat that was moored in the draw dock and then running out to the stem, where the water was deeper, jumping or diving in. However, when the crew returned they made us get out of the water so that they could leave, it was then that I noticed that I had a bright green stomach!

One of the men gave me a handful of cotton waste soaked in paraffin to help remove the paint, yet apart from adding to the smell it spread the area affected and left me a lot of explaining to do that night, for it was Friday, the night we had to use a tin bath in the kitchen of our home (not having the luxury of a bathroom). My posterior was a nice tinge of red by the time I got to bed, and needless to say I did not climb on freshly painted boats again, green or any other colour.

At last, then, I found myself along with my cousin Harry in the hall of the Worshipful Company of Watermen and Lightermen at St Mary-at-Hill in the City of London, a building steeped in history and traditions dating back to the days of the Tudors. Here we were sworn in, to serve our masters at all times, not to absent ourselves from their services for a period of seven years, during which time we were not to haunt play houses or taverns, nor contract matrimony, nor commit fornication (I had to ask dad what that meant).

Staring round the hall, where the Master and other court officials were resplendent in their badges of office, I was intrigued to see a large heraldic notice with the words, 'TIME AND TIDE WAIT FOR NO MAN', a motto that stuck in my mind from that day: no words can be more profound. An opportunity missed is lost forever, something that could alter one's whole life. I have missed a few in my time, and yet, I would not change one thing in the way my life has panned out. I am content, what more could one ask?

I rarely saw my master during the first two years of my apprenticeship, during which time I was to learn the rudiments of my trade, and appear at the hall once more to apply to be examined and for my licence to be granted, thus enabling me to work alone on the tideway. My first job afloat was for Messrs John Hawkins, of Lower Road, Rotherhithe. Alas, like so many other companies that once flourished on the Thames, they are now just another memory of long ago.

I was to report to that office on the following Monday morning at 8.00 a.m., and there at the given hour, I was met by a grey dumpling of a man, about five feet five inches in height, and almost the same in circumference. This was Joe Hull, senior foreman and labour-master for the firm that owned a fleet of some three craft towing tugs and a hundred lighters and canal barges, used in the conveyance of timber and other forestry produce to all parts of the tidal Thames, its docks, and the canal systems adjacent to this famous and historic waterway.

Joe, as he was affectionately known by all the workforce, said, 'I suppose you have got your union card lad', 'Yes Mr Hull' I answered, having been accepted at my local union branch on the previous Friday evening. Whilst there, I was furnished with a pamphlet setting out the current wages and conditions for each year of an apprentices service. I was to start at the princely sum of four shillings and four pence for an eight-hour day, and if overtime was incurred, this would net me ten pence per hour – in those far off days that was a very fair wage.

After that first morning my regular start time was nearly always 6.00 a.m. at the lock of the Surrey Canal, where I would be assisting in moving barges through the lock from the Surrey Commercial Docks, prior to pulling them a mile or so along the canal to their respective destinations, or moving the unladen (or 'light') barges from the canal basin back into the dock where a small tug would collect them in a long string, one behind the other, and tow them around the dock system, placing them at the various ships where they would collect their fresh parcels of timber ready to be delivered to some distant wharf or timber yard. The Surrey Commercial Docks was the largest timber import dock of its day. Originally it began life as 'Howlands' great dock, built to shelter shipping waiting in the Thames until they could be discharged at one of the Excise or Crown wharves. It was later owned by a whaling company where the whale oil and other products were brought ashore, a trade reflected in the name of the Greenland Dock, which was the main and largest part of the Surrey Dock system. I was informed that the jawbone of a whale was uncovered during the excavations made at the time of the construction of the Greenland Dock entrance, but I am getting ahead of myself.

Having picked up any fresh orders from the office, Joe bid me to follow him. We crossed over the cobbled road with its twin sets of tramlines – these carried the large double decked trams on their journey from the City of London, out to Woolwich and Abbey Wood, then back again, a journey then would have cost four pence, something less than two pence in today's money – and entered a large gateway with a notice in large letters above it, SURREY COMMERCIAL DOCKS, and in slightly smaller letters, Principal Entrance. Here Joe was nodded through by the very large police officer who was on duty in the gatehouse. These officers were employed by the Port of London Authority, and had all the powers of arrest etc. within the Port of London Authority's premises. This forms a very large section of London's east end, both to the north and south of the river, in addition to the powers of the Metropolitan Police or County Force within which this group of docks jurisdiction lay.

I was to be challenged by these officers quite often until they got to know me as an apprentice with good reasons to be within the dock areas. I followed Joe up the steep incline that led to the corner of a large dock, where I was to see the fantastic sight of ten or more ships, flying ensigns of almost as many different countries, laden or in the act of discharging cargoes of timber. Each ship was surrounded by barges either waiting to load or being loaded with freshly cut timber, mostly deal from the Scandinavian and Baltic countries, though there were a couple of ships carrying Canadian pine and cedar. The pungent aroma of the different wood was fresh on the nostrils like a 'well known' after-shave.

There was timber as far as the eye could see. A lot of it was floating on the surface of the water where it had been dislodged from the large stacks that these craft seemed to carry above deck level. On the other hand, some of the larger baulks of timber had been lashed and chained together by skilled 'rafters' who seemed to balance themselves on the long pile-like lengths whilst stapling them together with long lengths of coir or grass rope.

Once they had a couple lashed together they were able to pull the other lengths towards them as they were lowered over the ships side into the water. They would then take a staple from a canvas pouch tied around their waist and with an axe that had a hammer head on its reverse side, knock in a fresh staple to secure each new length of timber, first ensuring that the forward end of the raft that was being produced was straight and level. Thus a raft some fifteen feet in breadth and up to sixty feet or more long was made ready for towing to another part of the Surrey Docks where it would remain until required for the construction of some jetty or pier on the river.

On a smaller scale, there were two other men on a basic wooden raft of some seven or eight feet in width and approximately twenty feet long, pulling out driftwood and lengths of timber that had fallen into the dock from the many barges surrounding the ships. These would be eventually moved to the Surrey Canal basin where it would be landed to dry out in stacks and then sold as salvaged timber at reduced cost.

Whilst following on Joe's heels, I had to duck under lengths of planks stretched over large wooden trestles forming double gangways that ran from barges moored at the quay-side, up into the large sheds that extended on either side of the dock. Along these at regular intervals I could see muscular timber-porters wearing a felt hat with a leather shoulder shield attached, carrying large lengths of timber up into the sheds where they would be stored and seasoned in stacks that were some twenty feet high.

I was fascinated by the sort of 'spring heeled dance' that they developed as they moved over the bouncing planks, a sort of rhythmic bounce that carried them along as though they were floating on air.

Once they had deposited their load they would return on the parallel walkway passing their laden colleagues on the way up from the barge. I was hard-pressed to keep up with Joe, as he made his way along the quay side, and keep a look out for the many obstructions that encumbered the gap between the stowage areas and ships discharging their loads overside on to the quay, or into barges moored alongside.

It was to one of these ships that Joe made his first call. Here he spoke to one of the lightermen who was an employee of Hawkins and responsible for the safe loading of some of the company's barges that were receiving cargo from that ship. He would be given the position of the particular parcel on the ships manifest so that in conjunction with the shipworker, 'a person designated by the Ship's agents', he could have his barge ready for loading and alongside that particular hold when required. Thus preventing a hold-up in the offloading of the vessel. Also the dockers who were on piece-work would be a little upset if the delay cost them money.

The average freight loaded into these craft would total eighty to a hundred tons of timber or hardwood logs. Loading time varied depending on stowage requirements. The usual time per barge was about an hour. There were some three or four ships moored along this particular quay of Station Yard on the Canada Dock. We had joined it at clock house corner and moved along to each one where company craft were loading to check on craft requirements finally to find our selves at station corner of the dock and then to turn left along Station Quay and to a swing bridge that spanned a cutting that led into the Greenland Dock.

The bridge carried the Redriff Road which ran from Lower Road down to the riverside where at Redriff, a part of Rotherhithe and a very active part of the riverside wharfs and dry-docks where even an Isolation Hospital shared the river front, a well populated community was established.

At the bridge we saw a small tug, built with very low lines that would enable it to pass under the bridge with inches to spare when not encumbered with craft in tow, with a long string of laden barges attached waiting for the bridge to swing so that it could proceed on its way through the Greenland Dock by way of the cutting down to the locks leading into the river or to the canal. This tug, named the *Hawk* was owned by the company and was skippered at that time by Dave Hawkins, a nephew of the owner.

In less than six months I was to become boy mate with him on the *Hawk*, but before then I had a lot to learn about lightering and working afloat. After some three months of working in tandem with another young apprentice, Alf Carter, who like myself hailed from Stepney and shared the job of hauling the laden barges along the Grand Surrey Canal to their destined wharf where they were to be unloaded (sometimes a distance of two or three miles from the docks). Whilst completing these tasks I began to develop a few muscles and to fill out.

I enjoyed the life and looked forward to the time when I would be able to obtain my Apprentice's Licence which would enable me to work on the tideway without supervision. This however would be after two years of hard work, six months of which was spent as boy mate of the *Hawk*, the little dock tug previously mentioned, along with Dave Hawkins as my Skipper.

It was very hard work. Not only had I to keep the tug spotless with all the brasswork gleaming – a job that seemed endless in itself – but I had to hand out tow ropes, throw out lines to craft that were just beyond the reach of the tug and quickly make them fast to a small round bollard that the towing hook was secured to. When I say make it fast, one had to throw on a 'back' turn, then three 'round' turns in very quick time as the little tug surged forward under the strain of her powerful little engine. Then it was stand by to throw off the turns and take in the slack as the engine was put in reverse as the tow was pulled clear, then repeat the performance until the barge was close enough to throw a 5 foot tow rope to the lighterman for him to make fast to the towing bitts.

I became very adept at throwing the break out line as we called it. It consisted of a 2 foot 5 inch Manilla rope some twenty fathoms in length with a bowline eye at the end, a spliced eye was of no use as the eye would close the moment it left the hand, whereas the bowline knotted eye would remain open until it settled around the bollard where it was intended to be – at least that was the theory. I could hit the mark nine times out of ten by the time I left the *Hawk* and started learning new skills. I'm afraid that there are also many times that I have put that skill to good use when recovering people from a watery grave.

My next lessons were to be driving lessons; not in motor vehicles, but in the art of using the tide to navigate the barge with the aid of a long pair of sweeps or oars from anywhere on the tideway to destinations where the craft was required. My tutor was a very spritely sixty-year-old by the name of Jimmy Rae and the very first lesson began when we undocked from the Surrey entrance of the Surrey Commercial Docks at Rotherhithe on an early flood tide.

We eased the barge out into mid-stream and commenced our journey upriver. Our destination was Putney Drawdock some ten nautical miles further upriver. The barge we were driving was a mere 'punt' as we termed the smaller barges. She was some twenty tons registered and would carry thirty to thirty-five tons of timber, carefully stowed in the hold space so that we would have a level 'floor' to walk across should we require to move the sweep from forward to aft as required.

We had not progressed very far when a light mist formed over the river at not more than about eight to ten feet in depth, this was a bit disconcerting as we were hidden from some of the larger vessels that were still underway though proceeding slowly. One in particular, a small coaster belonging to the General Steam Navigation Company, suddenly loomed out the mist bound downriver and less than ten yards away. Fortunately for us there was a lookout in the bows who spotted us in time enabling a warning to be given to the bridge personnel allowing them to alter course enough for them to slide past us with a couple of feet to spare.

I was extremely pleased to see the fog had lifted by the time we were abreast of the Thames Division's police pier at Wapping. We were making fair headway, keeping as far as possible in the main flow of the tide. As Jimmy said, 'Keep your head up to the points, and you won't get swept into the bights.' A swim-headed barge will always trade ahead – it had something to do with the fixed budget (a steel rudder-like structure under the after cabin area).

The river in those days, just prior to the Second World War, was a very busy place. The riverside wharfs were a hive of industry with ships mostly from the continent, Scandinavia and Scotland. There was a regular weekly service from Leith into the Upper Pool, so the comings and goings were almost an hourly event on the rising tide. Ships desiring the bascules of Tower Bridge to be raised had to fly a special signal when passing Cherry Garden Pier, thus enabling the bridge keepers to halt the road traffic on the approaches to the bridge in good time to prevent accidents.

In those far-off days, the traffic consisted mostly of horse-drawn carts and open lorries that rarely exceeded any speed limits. Our progress was steady, being early on the tide there were very few tugs and tows at that stage to be encumbered by our slow progress through the bridges. The regular standby tug at Tower Bridge was not required to pull us clear of any inward or outbound shipping, this being their main requirement, so our progress past the Tower Gardens was unhindered. I cannot remember whether there was an Eagle Steamer lying at Tower Pier – this was usually where the excursions to Southend, Ramsgate, and Margate began, returning upriver some twelve hours later. The bars would be open as soon as the vessel got under way. You can imagine that they were very popular.

Onward through the old London Bridge with its five arches and flanked on the north upper side by the Fishmongers Hall and the home of that Liveried and Ancient Guild, through the Cannon Street, Southwark and Blackfriars bridges we steadily made our progress, keeping to the centre of the arches to avoid hitting the cambers or buttresses where applicable, until we approached Waterloo Bridge where the old structure was being demolished to make way for the new bridge which was to have just three spans.

Here we were collected by the attendant tug who towed us clear of the workings and the Coffer-dams surrounding the new and old footings where men were working below the waterline. We went on up through Hungerford Charring Cross Railway Bridge, Hungerford being the foot bridge on the lower or downstream side. This was the site of Brunel's suspension bridge which spanned the river using the two brick abutments that still exist, though the one on the north shore has been incorporated into the embankment built by Sir Joseph Bazelegate at the time when a lot of London's old rivers such as the Fleet and Tyburn were incorporated into the sewerage system taking it many miles downriver to Beckton outfall, just above Barking Creek where the River Roding joins the Thames.

With the coming of the Railways, Brunel's bridge was dismantled and reassembled as the Clifton Suspension Bridge down in the West Country, thus allowing the all powerful railway Companies to use the site for their own purposes. I know that I am digressing, but who could resist talking about this wonderful and historic river of ours when passing upstream through the City of London and of

Westminster? We must press on, however, and continue our drive up through Westminster Bridge with its seven arches and where skill was needed to avoid the fairly sharp butments and low headroom – in fact just 5.4 metres at high water on a spring tide.

This of course was of no danger to us, but has to be looked at very carefully by the skippers of some of the larger pleasure craft to ensure they have room to pass under on a rising tide. Here, the Palaces of Westminster, with their magnificent gothic buildings, stretch along the north shore. On the south side of the river and just down stream from Lambeth Bridge, lies Lambeth Palace once the home of the wife of King Henry VIII, Anne of Cleves. This is now the official home of Archbishop of Canterbury.

Through Lambeth Bridge, with its pineapple mounted plinths adorning the balustrades on either side, and passing the home of the London Fire Brigade on the south shore and the famous 'Massey Shaw' fire float moored to their pier, the latter was to do some sterling work at Dunkirk during the evacuations in the May of 1940. We went onwards through Vauxhall Bridge with its magnificent statues adorning the abutments on either side. Victoria Railway Bridge and Chelsea Bridge were soon to follow then a longer stretch up to the Albert Suspension Bridge, again another fairly low bridge.

We seemed to be making good progress and the river traffic had eased. Most of the tugs and tows bound for Brentford and beyond had long since overtaken us and faded into the distance. A laden collier of the 'flat iron' variety, slipped by on his way to Fulham Power Station. The berth there had been vacated much earlier just as soon as there was sufficient water to enable the previous tenant to proceed downriver whilst he still had sufficient clearance to allow him to pass under the bridges on the rising tide.

Victoria railway and Battersea Bridges were soon negotiated leaving just Wandsworth, Putney rail, and Putney Bridge, and then we were there. By this time the incoming tide had slackened and we were having to put more effort into making headway. Fortunately for us there was a tug in attendance at Wandsworth Bridge where the new bridge was in its final stages of being completed. The centre section still had to be put in position. The tug took us in tow and gave us a good start toward our destination; we had almost made it when the tide started to ebb. We went through the Railway Bridge and were almost there. Jim was just about ready to drop down to the buoys in Wandsworth Reach to moor up for the night, when a police boat appeared from upriver and seeing our plight gave us a tow. He had to slip the tow fairly quickly, but not before giving us enough headway to enable us reach our berth. I have always held our river police in high regard since that day. With a friendly wave they went on their way.

By the time we moored our craft and went ashore, we were very grateful for a cup of tea and a sausage sandwich at the coffee stall by the drawdock. My hands were red and blistered and my arms felt like lead; I was ready to take the long journey home from Putney Bridge to Mile End on the underground. How I managed to wake up in time to leave the train at my station, I've no idea. I felt like sleeping for a week.

That was my first of many driving Lessons with Jim. We covered most parts of the river between Barking in the east and Putney in the west including Barking, Bow and Chelsea Creeks. He was a natural-born waterman who taught me a great deal without me realising just how much I was absorbing. I think my employers knew that Jim was the best, which is why every apprentice coming up for his two's was sent out with Jim for a few lessons.

Needless to say, I managed to pass my examination at Waterman's Hall that September. Yes, the very month that war was declared and everything changed for many of us.

# CHAPTER TWO

# LICENSED APPRENTICE

With the coming of the war, many things altered. The blackout caused quite a few accidents within the dock areas and on the craft resulting in a few accidental drownings. Some of this was overcome by painting a broad white strip along the edge of the quays and along the outer edge of the gunwhales of the barges and lighters. All the bollards and other possible obstructions were similarly treated. Navigation lights had to be screened to prevent them from being seen by aircraft. Similarly any headlights had to be covered or painted over.

A great deal of the regular shipping that used to bring timber in from overseas was halted. So the company that I was employed by had to lay off some of the hands. Apprentices could only be employed if there were at least four Freemen Lightermen for each apprentice actually in work. This was to prevent them being used as cheap labour. As we were all employed on a daily basis, this would mean that we would have to appear outside the office at 5.00 p.m. each evening to see if there was sufficient work for employment the following day.

There was no payment for this; however it was the only way that you could get employment. The term for this was 'being on the stones'. It was finally agreed by the employers that the apprentices could work a week on and a week off alternately. I was in a bit of a cleft stick: I could not draw unemployment pay because I was too young, and I was still expected to pay my way at home. So I ventured to try out another lighterage company who dealt in carrying copra and palm kernels – these were essential in the manufacture of margarine and cooking fats. The copra was usually rancid, oozing a slippery film over the gunwhales making it very dangerous to walk along them whilst under way behind some of the more powerful tugs.

One occasion I was sent down to Tilbury Dock to undock a barge that had discharged a similar cargo. It was midnight and pitch black and I had difficulty moving about on her decks. Along with several other craft we were taken in tow by one of Gaselee's Tugs – this was a towing company that was hired by lighterage firms to undertake towing their craft for them and were commonly known as 'Seeking Tugs'. Once the tow got under way you were on your own. The after cabin was very damp and I had difficulty in finding enough material to light a fire in the little stove so I spent a rather miserable night until we reached the entrance to the Millwall Dock in early hours of the morning, then, as soon as we were locked in and I found the ship to which I was to deliver the barge, I went to the nearest coffee shop for a hot cup of tea and something to eat.

Lightermen shifting barges into Hays Dock. The barges had come from Tilbury Dock loaded with chests of tea.

On my return to the barge I encountered one the Company's Freemen who wanted to know why I had not folded up the tarpaulins laying in the hold and placed them up on the deck ready for use. I told him that I had spent a cold and hungry night without a drink, and that was my first priority, now if he wanted a hand I would be happy to help him. If he had any complaints it should be with the lazy so-and-so who was in charge when the barge was unloaded in Tilbury Dock. He complained to the office and I found myself back 'on the stone's'.

My next employer was a company that were employed in the transport of chilled meat and similar products. This Company had its own tugs with crews who looked after the hands with a cup of tea and sometimes, 'no questions asked', a small joint of lamb to help out with the rations at home. I was with this company for some three months before I was laid off again. The following evening I went up to the City where this company's office was located and was waiting outside with several other hopefuls when a Mr. Harry Hill, the Labour Master for F. T. EVERARD & Sons, came over to us and announced that he was looking for four hands for immediate start with a guaranteed twelve months work.

He was almost knocked down in the rush. I had a job to convince him that I was old enough, and he checked with his office to see if they had sufficient Freemen employed to put me on the books. For a few anxious moments I had to wait before getting a nod. I had nearly a whole year working for this company and the job I liked most was being Wharf Bosun up on the Grand Union Canal at Southall, where I was responsible for delivering canal barges to Messrs. Poulton & Noel, laden with navy beans to be turned into baked beans.

I used to collect the craft from Brentford Dock and tow them up to Southall behind a horse; there were a number of locks to negotiate including the Hanwell Flight. This was a series of seven locks one after the other and needed a little skill in controlling the barge in order to prevent damage to the lock gates. Once these had been negotiated and the craft were safely in the Maypole Dock, it was a matter of uncovering and removing the hatches and leaving the work force to remove the beans. The dock was roofed over so that there was no need for my presence until it was time to bring the barge away and return it down to Brentford Dock for return to the river.

I suppose that I must have spent a good few weeks at Southall. When not required at the dock I would have a look around Hayes, a nearby area, with the lad whose father owned and operated the stable of horses that carried out the towing along that section of the canal. I once went with him to an auction where cars were up for bidding; at that time, petrol was rationed and a lot of the owners had been called up, so there were a number of bargains to be had. In fact I could have bought an Austin Chummy Seven for as little as two pounds ten shillings, a sum that was equivalent to half of my average weekly earnings at that time. I did see a Singer Le Mans Sports Tourer, less than four years old, go for as little as four pounds ten shillings; as there had been no retainer put on the vehicle, it was sold for that knock-down price, leaving the previous owner in tears.

I vowed to get a car for myself at the next auction, but unfortunately my father had to go into hospital at that time with result that I became the bread-winner for the next week or two, and by the time that he had recovered, my job at Southall had come to an end.

One of the barges that I had previously brought down from Southall to Brentford had to be towed down to Millwall Dock leaving sometime after 11.00 p.m. It was a very cold night so I made sure that I had sufficient coal for the fire. This was fairly easy to manage as the barge was lying next to a coal wharf where several select pieces of hard steam coal were lying dangerously close to the edge of the quay, so I thought that I ought to remove the hazard to prevent an accident. Yet again we were using another seeking tug for the tow downriver and I did not expect to reach my destination till about four in the morning, so once under way I settled in the tiny cabin enjoying the warmth of the hot little stove before nodding off. I think that it must have been the sound of the tug's whistle that aroused me when blowing the signal for rounding at Millwall Dock. As I got to my feet I felt a sharp pain in the big toe of my right foot; clutching the painful area, a portion of my shoe came away in my hand. It had literally burnt away. I must have had my shoe resting against the stove for several hours.

Coming up on deck from the tiny cabin I received another shock. It had been snowing and at least three inches of snow covered the ground. I had to hobble around in an effort to prevent my toe touching the ground, and managed to secure my barge to others that were waiting to lock in to the dock, I then tried to find a piece canvas to cover my toe cap and the sole of my shoe. Eventually I found an old torn tarpaulin that was ready to donate a useful section, and with the aid of a few lashings I was able to create a barrier against the icy carpet of snow. I managed to get my barge to where it was required for loading in the dock then made my way home drawing a few curious looks on the way. What really hurt was the fact that I had only recently purchased the shoes in Petticoat Lane the previous Sunday.

We were now into early 1940, probably around late February or early March. The war seemed far away; I think that there had been one or two occasions when the sirens had sounded, but there was very little activity in the air over London at that time. However, things were soon to change with the break through into the Low Countries, the capitulation of Belgium, soon followed by the fall of the Maginot Line and then Dunkirk.

Many small vessels, tugs, sailing barges, pleasure cruisers and private craft made their way downriver to be organised into a ferrying service in an endeavour to get our lads off the beaches and safely home. I would have loved to have gone but was not given the opportunity. I had two of my uncles serving in France; they were amongst the lucky ones to make it back.

I stayed in employment with Everards for some time, working down the lower reaches of the Thames around the Greenhithe and Purfleet cement manufacturing areas. Everards had contracts for the conveyance of cement to a number of places in the upper reaches from the Tunnel Cement Works at Purfleet. Whilst I was down in that area I was privileged to witness some of the dogfights that took place over Essex and Kent as our 'gallant few' met and fought off the Luftwaffe. To them we owe a debt that money alone cannot pay.

As we got further into the year, several bombing sorties by the Luftwaffe took place over London but it was not until the September of that year that we truly knew what bombing really was. I was at home on the Saturday 7 September. Normally I should have been working in the docks, however as I was still an apprentice and there were insufficient Freemen employed on that day, so I was laid off until the following Monday. I had spent a fairly quiet morning catching up on a couple of jobs in the house and was preparing to get myself ready to go out round about midday.

It was fine, warm and sunny, an ideal day to go over to Victoria Park with an old school pal. My mother had gone to the front door of the house which faced east. 'Come and have a look at this son,' she called. I went to the pavement where she was standing out in the front of the house and looked up to see formations of light grey aircraft, fairly high, approaching our area. I cannot remember hearing an air-raid warning, but soon we observed the ack-ack bursts in the sky around or in the general direction of the planes followed by the sound of distant explosions. 'I think that we had better get in the shelter mum,' I said. We had an Anderson shelter in the garden next door; it was the only place that did not have a concrete yard, and our neighbours had evacuated leaving us to look after their property whilst allowing us to place our shelter in their garden which was reached by a gate in the back fence by the privies – the latter were an essential item to our shelter life for many nights to come.

The explosions were getting nearer. Dad and I had fashioned a couple of bunks in the shelter and a fairly stout door; thankfully it was dry. The bombing continued for some hours as wave after wave came over. The ground beneath the shelter seemed to bounce and I felt as though I was on board a boat in a rough sea.

Mum was beginning to worry that my father had not arrived home. He was due about 1.00 p.m. having left his work in Woolwich Arsenal at midday, walking through the subway to North Woolwich and then catching a train to Burdett Road Station which was about two hundred yards away. This normally took him about an hour; today would be very different and we were to spend nearly four hours in the shelter before there was a lull and we could take stock.

As we emerged from the shelter we could hear fire engine bells going in every direction; there was a pall of smoke rising from the general direction of the docks and a strong smell of burning. There seemed to be a stunned silence in the immediate neighbourhood, as the shock set in, then people emerged from wherever they had been sheltering to look around, taking in the rising plumes of smoke and dust around the dock areas.

We had been lucky in that our immediate area had little or no damage, except odd bits of shrapnel damage, which cracked a few tiles here and there. Everyone started to talk at once: 'Are you alright?' 'Have you seen my Son or Daughter?' as the case may be.

Mum was really worried that my father had not arrived home. It was not until some two hours or more that he appeared looking tired and dishevelled, his clothing and hair coated in a film of grey dust. Mum just ran and hugged him with tears of relief steaming down her cheeks.

When he could speak he said, 'I could murder a cup of tea, my throat is that parched, I could not spit to save my life.' When he had managed to down half the pot of tea that I had made for us, he told us what had happened, though not before saying how relieved and happy he was to see that we were okay and that the house was still standing. It appeared that he had boarded the train okay at North Woolwich Station and it had made its way via Custom House, Canning Town, Plaistow, and Stratford Stations without any problems.

It was when they reached Bow Road Station, just one station away from his stop at Burdett Road, that the train was stopped on the high level bridge that spanned Bow Road. Here they were told to get out and take shelter. Bombs were already falling around the area as they made their way to a surface shelter on the other side of Bow Road. Dad had to walk, or rather run, by what appeared to him an open manhole on the corner of the pavement outside the Police Station. He made the shelter with just a few seconds to spare when a blast propelled him further into the interior and a wall of thick choking dust filled the shelter leaving many of the people inside to believe they were under a Gas attack.

What worried my father most was the plume of white steam emanating from the stopped engine of the train on the bridge. Being an artillery man from the First World War, he thought that it would be a well-defined target for the bombers. It was some time before the shelter warden thought that it was safe enough for them to emerge from the shelter, so when they eventually came out and had a look around, my father was shocked to see that the corner of the Bow Road Police Station had collapsed. The open manhole that he had passed on his way to the shelter was in fact caused by a delayed action bomb that had detonated as he was entering the shelter.

Seven police officers who were sheltering in the basement at that time were killed together with others who were severely injured. Dad advised my mother to go to stay with a relation living in Reading, taking my younger sister who had been evacuated to somewhere near

Woking with her. Mum went the next day, but not before having to endure one of the worst nights of the Blitz, where the bombers came back guided by the huge inferno of the Surrey Docks where millions of tons of timber were destroyed. Wharfs and warehouses were ablaze all along the riverside; complete havoc reigned everywhere.

The bombers were relentless; it was not until the dawn that the 'All Clear' sounded. Sleep only arrived through sheer exhaustion. Some windows had to be boarded up, though this was not big a problem as it helped with the blackout which was strictly imposed. One house that fronted on to Burdett Road by the Fire Station was broken into to extinguish a bedroom light that had been left on. The residents had sought shelter in the underground railway stations.

I don't think that there was any looting at that time; we did not live in a very affluent area, in fact in those days most houses had a piece of string that led through a hole in the middle of the door attached to the latch or lock – with one pull you were in. The only person who was not welcome was the 'Tally Man' who, when expected, got the string withdrawn, or, 'Sorry, mum's out,' from the kids. That Sunday morning dad saw mum off at Mile End Station; she would not let him go with her any further on her way to Reading. On his return home, we set about making the shelter a little more habitable with some bedding, blankets and an improvised cupboard for storing tea, sugar and condensed milk.

We had rigged a substantial cable from the power supply, enabling us to use an electric kettle and a small radiant fire that was useful to make pieces of toast. I don't suppose for one minute that it would have met with today's safety requirements but to us, during the next coming months when the nightly visitations by 'Jerry' left us with little time to spend in the comfort of the house, it served. Mostly it was 'work and shelter'. The underground trains were still running, but my father had to cycle to Woolwich on a number of occasions.

Depending where I was required I could normally get there on time remembering that 'time and tide' waited for no one – especially on a falling tide. If you were not there when the tug called, it was another twelve or more hours before you could get under way; this was something that the bosses did not want to easily understand. Moving about on buses was not always the easiest form of transport as many roads were criss-crossed with fire hoses, where weary-looking firemen with soot-blackened faces were still struggling to contain fires and having to find undamaged hydrants where water was still obtainable.

Each and every day revealed more damaged areas. Sometimes you would pass the incredible sight of a solitary wall standing with a clock and other ornaments still on the mantle shelf; the fireplace with the rest of the house just rubble in the basement. Here there would be rescue squads digging away, endeavouring to rescue or recover the bodies of the inhabitants. Other areas had barricades across the road or street with the sign 'unexploded bomb' and a Royal Engineers twenty-five-hundred-weight truck outside, with red painted mudguards with the words 'bomb disposal' painted on the tailboard.

On one occasion I saw a shirt-sleeved sapper, with his sleeves rolled up and braces showing, walk out of the front door of a house, a big grin on his face, carrying a bomb on his shoulder. This he walked to the truck and placed it between a couple of sandbags to prevent it rolling about, then off he drove with a young army officer who had followed him out of the house. I understand that they often took them out to Hackney Marshes, where they destroyed them by using a controlled explosive.

These lads deserved all the medals that they were awarded during the war. It took nerves of steel to do the tricky jobs that they encountered day after day. One such job was the recovery of a bomb that had failed to explode in the Surrey Docks, it had penetrated the roadway some twenty-five feet from the water's edge and had gone well down into the subsoil. A pump was needed to keep the hole free of water which was seeping in. Every time they managed to expose the tail-fins of the bomb, it had sunk a little more into the mud. Eventually they were able to rig some tackle around the fins sufficiently to prevent it sinking any further into the subsoil, and also to shore up the sides of the hole to prevent it collapsing in on the officer who had the onerous task of removing the fuse, making the bomb safe for removal.

This job seemed to take weeks of hard work; it makes one wonder how many more remain undiscovered in Docklands. I often had to go to our company's offices in Great Tower Street, where I got on very well with the office manager who would pass on my orders for my next day's work. I think that his name was Mr. Sanderson, but he was known to one and all as 'Sandy', a very cheerful, well-liked man who treated all the lightermen and us apprentices with respect.

I was stunned to learn a few weeks later that Sandy had been killed when his house took a direct hit. I suppose it brought home to all of us that death was a possibility at any time. I have previously mentioned the Tunnel Cement works at Purfleet from where we had quite a lot of freight. Everards had a fairly modern fleet of lighters that had a capacity of four hundred and thirty tons burden load. With cement, this would be lost in the hold space under the hatches; this was always in one hundredweight paper bags evenly spaced across the hold.

There also were lighters of the same length and breadth, though not so deep drafted, that were used to convey freights of cement to a wharf at Brentford where the berth had not the depth of water to accommodate the larger craft. On one occasion I was ordered to be at Brentford together with a Freeman Lighterman to man two of these unladen lighters to be towed down to Purfleet behind a tug belonging to Messrs. Clement Knowling, this was a well-established towing company on the river, whose moorings were at Brentford.

The tugs were coal-burning steam engined vessels of a considerable age, fairly reliable, though not over-fast. The trip down on the ebb tide took over six hours and on our arrival at Purfleet we had to walk nearly a mile to a canteen for a meal. We then returned to find two laden lighters to be towed back to Brentford behind the same tug. It was about 2.00 p.m. by the time we left Purfleet on our way back upriver. We made fairly slow progress as the craft were deep in the water with approximately two hundred and seventy tons in each barge. We had reached somewhere about Westminster Bridge when the sirens sounded. It was dusk and we were beginning to lose the light. There was very little that we could do about it but press on, though I think that the skipper of the tug was wishing he had a proper wheelhouse with a steel roof like some of the tugs working in the lower reaches. Unfortunately for him, his had to be collapsible in order to negotiate the low bridges in the upper reaches. As it grew dark we could hear some ack-ack guns downriver and a few explosions in the distance. Still we pressed on, reaching Putney Bridge at about 10.00 p.m. The activity grew nearer by the minute, with ack-ack guns firing all around. At that point we could not leave the craft anywhere as there were no convenient moorings to be had. We were just clear of Hammersmith Bridge when the skipper decided that he'd had enough. He informed us that he was going to leave us at the council wharf at Chiswick, where we could safely stay until he came back for us on the morning tide.

It was after midnight before there was sufficient water to get the craft alongside, during which time shrapnel was falling all around. We kept down in the after cabin of one of the lighters during the worst of these periods; this was the one furthest away from the wharf, when there was a loud bang as something hit the edge of the deck followed by the sound of something hot going into the cold river. An oil bomb had just clipped our quarter and luckily for us was extinguished before it could do any damage, though it did leave a large indent on the edge of the deck.

As soon as the craft were safely moored we had a walk ashore. We knew that it was too late to catch a train; it was fairly dark but as our eyes got used to the night we espied a low building and just for a moment a chink of light as a door was opened and just as quickly closed.

We made our way there and knocked on the door. It was opened by a woman dressed in the uniform of the Auxiliary Fire Service. We were quickly brought into the warmth of what was a fire station. Having told the firemen of our predicament and of the fact that we had been without food and a cup of tea for nearly twelve hours, we were given a feed of bacon sandwiches and a mug of tea, and then they found a berth for us in the pit below the engine where we snuggled down for the night.

The following day was a Saturday. The barges were still aground until midday, Bill and I went to a nearby cafe for our breakfast and then returned to the wharf to await the return of the tug to complete the tow up to Brentford. Several tugs towing craft passed by on their way upriver, including one belonging to Clement Knowling, but they passed with no indication that they would be coming back for us.

Bill went on the phone to the foreman, the office being closed on a Saturday, but was told to return to the craft and wait. I was at the wharf the whole time on standby. Still no tug arrived. Eventually the tide began to ebb and there was no way that we would be able to berth the craft in the dock at Brentford.

When we contacted the office on the Monday morning, we were informed that a tug had called and that we were nowhere to be found, with the result that we were to be laid off. I had to assure Bill that I had not left the wharf at any time, and that the firemen who were there on duty could confirm this.

We lost four day's work over this incident until I went to the union and explained our case. We had been left at the wharf all night, so we certainly did not wish to stay there any longer. I'm pleased to say that the firemen confirmed this. So when we were eventually seen by Mr William Everard at the Great Tower Street Office together with our union man, we were reinstated immediately. Shortly after this incident, my house in Wager Street, Burdett Road, suffered substantial damage during the night. Dad and I were in the shelter when we heard a 'whistling' bomb – Jerry used a lot of these during the Blitz to unnerve people – on its way down. It seemed to get louder and louder so much so that I shook my fathers hand and said, 'I think this is the one dad.'

It very nearly was the end: when daylight came and we looked out of the shelter, we could see that the corner of the house and most of the roof had collapsed. I rang the foreman to get my job covered, and arranged to get some tarpaulins to cover the furniture that survived the blast. My uncle's house at Leytonstone was made available to us. He was in the Army, and my aunt was evacuated with her two young daughters. I loaded some of our more precious items including our radiogram, onto a barrow and pushed it for some six or seven miles to our new abode. We stayed there for approximately five nights. My elder Sister Rose who was then a conductress on the trolleybuses turned up with her husband Alf, who had leave from the Navy before joining another ship.

As they had only been married in August of 1939, and had only spent a few months together before he was called up, we allowed them the Anderson shelter in my uncle's garden in which to hold their reunion. Dad and I used the one next door where the occupants were away. At 2.00 a.m. the wooden door that we had fashioned to keep the night air out, blew in upon us, and we heard the sound of shattering glass and rubble falling everywhere. It was a repetition of what we had experienced less than a week ago. When we went to see how my sister and her husband had got on, we were amazed to find them still happily unaware of their near miss. They were actually on the very edge of the crater left by the bomb, and what is more there was another Anderson shelter in the adjoining garden that was on the other side of the crater with people in it who had not felt a thing. It was uncanny as the blast had been directed upward and taken quite a bit of the roofing off and shattered the conservatory glass roof.

A decision was then made that we move out of London to a place in Essex. We chose South Benfleet, somewhere that I used to stay as a youngster with my cousins, where we found a house for rent that would accommodate our needs. My mother and younger sister joined us so that we were a reunited family again. My father continued to work in Woolwich Arsenal travelling by train to Barking Station, then continuing by cycle to Woolwich. I found that it was going to be difficult for me to continue working as a 'City' hand for Everards, also there was no way that I could get to Greenhithe where their Barge Yard and other office was located. So reluctantly I had to find other employment closer at hand.

I was offered a job at a chalk quarry in Grays; this was better than nothing though I missed the river, and I felt a little better when they asked me if I would like to work at their jetty. I was on the river as such, though the job I was given was trimming loam that was brought from the quarry and tipped from their trucks into the holds of small coasters. This was to ensure that they filled the hold spaces under the decks to reduce the chance of the cargo shifting at sea. I stuck with this job for some time; winter was on way and at least the job kept me warm and exercised my muscles, keeping me in trim.

I continued working there for a month or so when I was informed that work had fallen off and that I would be laid off. I had been travelling from Benfleet by bus during which time I had made friends with a chap who was invariably on the same bus every day. On mentioning to him that I was looking for employment again, he said that his firm who had the contract for building the blast walls around the oil tanks at Purfleet required labourers. I went along the next day where I joined a gang working behind a cement mixer and running concrete to the base of the tanks where foundations were being laid, or offloading breeze blocks or bricks from lorries. It was tough work on the hands until I fashioned some palm shields from some inner tube material.

The pay was by the hour: one shilling and five pence halfpenny. Eleven shillings and eightpence a day, providing it did not rain. If that happened the finished work was covered up to prevent the concrete mixture being weakened and we were laid off until it either stopped raining, or sent home if the hour was near finishing time. During one of these early lay-offs, I walked along to Purfleet Railway Station to see if that was a viable alternative to the bus from South Benfleet. Whilst there I noticed one of William Cory & Son's tugs lying at a coal jetty almost adjacent to the station. I walked out to the jetty to enquire if there were any vacancies either in the craft or on the jetty. I was advised to go up to the office to see the wharf manager and lighterage boss of the Purfleet Depot.

I was asked for my licence and union card and on production of these items, was welcomed with open arms to start on the following Monday night. The tug named *Redoubt* had three crews of eight men, i.e. skipper, a boy mate who was an unlicenced apprentice, a foreman lighterman, three more lightermen or licenced apprentices, an engineer and a fireman (the tug was a coal-burning steam vessel). We worked round the clock on twelve hours on and twenty-four hours off. Every third week it worked out that if the last day of the week fell on a Saturday, you would have to work on the Sunday day shift and again on the Monday day shift. This alternated the shifts and meant that the Sunday was at overtime rate.

Sunday nights were never worked except in exceptional circumstances. The work was based mainly around the jetty, moving empty barges from the barge roads to the ships that were being discharged at the jetty, and in turn removing them back to the roads when loaded to await collection by other tugs from the company's very large fleet that supplied London with coal for its power station, gasworks and factories all over the Metropolis. We also supplied to others further afield on the creeks and canals leading from the river.

There were three main jetties owned by the company: one at Purfleet, another at Erith and a larger one at Gallions by the Royal Docks. There were coaling hulks for the shipping in the river, which also supplied some of the larger coal burning passenger ships in the docks with coal bunkers with the aid of large floating bunkering unit.

William Cory's ships and tugs had a black diamond funnel mark on a white band. Their barges had a white diamond painted on the bows; this made it easy to pick out the craft at a distance.

I had come to another crossroad in my life, and I liked the feel of being back on the river again. Whilst I had been working ashore, a period of some six months, I had joined the Benfleet section of the Home Guard, formally known as the Local Defense Volunteers. I had done quite a bit of training with them, and thoroughly enjoyed the comradeship and valued the many friends that I had made whilst with them. So having seen my commanding officer who happened to be the local bank manager, (shades of Dad's Army), I made arrangements with them to parade as and when I could as fitted in with my shifts.

The first day I stepped on board and met up with my new workmates, I knew that I would fit in. The skipper was a man named Dick Stone, who lived in East Ham. The foreman was a chap by name of Joe Hardy, who resided in a house close to the Purfleet Station. His son Bill Hardy was of a similar age to myself and of the same year of apprenticeship. The other lighterman was a chap by the name of Olley Smith; he was around fifty-five or sixty years of age. He was very experienced, having been a sailing barge skipper in his younger days. I enjoyed many a yarn with Olley, he could name a sailing barge by the cut of its rig when it was a mile or so away. I have never found him to be wrong, and these were the days when the river was full of sailing barges.

The engineer, who hailed from Grays, was an ex-Royal Navy man by the name of George Stowers; his fireman, also ex-R.N., was Bill Freston. Where George was short and rotund, Bill was tall and lean but had the misfortune to suffer from foot trouble. I think that this could have been caused by standing and working in a hot evironment day after day. Though he did take the weight off once he had a good head of steam and the ashes had been cleared.

I must not forget the 'boy mate', Jimmy Jewiss, who came from Grays. Jim and I were to become lifelong friends. Jim's father was a lighterman who once worked for the Anglo American Oil Company, which had a fleet of tugs and tank barges working from their wharf at Purfleet. It would appear that he was lost overboard one night whilst boarding the tug from one of the barges whilst under way. Jim's mother was able to apprentice Jim as was her right being the widow of a freeman lighterman.

Jim's elder brother Ernie had been 'called up' and was then serving in the Inland Water Transport, a marine section of the Royal Engineers. At the time I joined the crew of the *Reboubt*, I was still known by my first Christian name; I had three in all.

When I was to be baptised, my mother wanted me to be called John William, after her two elder brothers and her father, my grandfather, whose name was John but known to every body as Jack. The change came about fairly early in my being a member of the crew. We had gathered some craft from the barge roads on the other side of Long Reach where the jetty was situated, and were towing them over to the inner side of the jetty on an ebb tide. So we had four barges, two in each column with towropes in the leading craft. Now depending on which side the skipper wanted craft to sheer out to enable him to let them pass as he came astern, he would call to the hand on the leading barge on that side to let go his tow rope, the mate would then quickly pull the tow rope in clear of the stern, so that the skipper could telegraph the engineer to put the engines in reverse, thus allowing the craft to slide past.

Alas, all he shouted was 'Let go Joe!' I obeyed the last order, little realising that the foreman's name was also Joe, and he was standing by the towrope on the other barge. I am not at all sure what names I was being called by the skipper, though I can imagine that the air was blue for sometime; like all tug skippers, they have a very good vocabulary. As soon as we were able to reconnect the tow and place the craft where they were supposed to go, and I had apologised to the skipper on returning aboard the tug, I was asked what other names I had, apart from those that the skipper had given me. And so I was called Jack from there on in.

It stuck with me on joining the Navy that Jim and I were going to be together for the first year of our service life. We still had to contend with air raids both day and night, and our enemy had taken to dropping mines in the river. These were of two types, acoustic and magnetic. The latter were dealt with by having degaussing facility set up at Tilbury landing stage where once a month the tugs and smaller vessels operating on the river who did not have their own degaussing system, were required to go alongside the pier to have a cable passed around the vessel. The vessel would then be 'wiped', as this process was termed. It meant that the magnetic field of the vessel would virtually be eliminated, thus lessening the chances of activating a magnetic mine.

Wooden minesweepers were working constantly in pairs towing a length of cable astern of each vessel and working in parallel to set up a magnetic field between the cables to activate any magnetic mine in its field. Also one of them would have a sonic boom strapped to its bow sending out a loud noise similar to that made by a pneumatic road drill. If you were in a cabin or space anywhere below the waterline, it would be possible to hear them a mile away. This was meant to activate the acoustic mines long before the sweeper reached the mine; however, even with all these precautions, quite a number of vessels were sunk or blown up. One in particular was a Saint Line Vessel of approximately 10,000 tons that arrived from the *Argentine* with grain to be discharged at Bellamy's Wharf, Rotherhithe. It was in the act of rounding to go alongside of the wharf when it struck the mine and sunk in the fairway.

Another and even greater tragedy was the sinking of an oil tanker just arrived from South America at Shell Oil Refinery, Thames Haven. Apparently it had berthed alongside one of the jetties at the refinery and someone had gone ashore to pick up mail for the ship's company. He was to be the only survivor, for someone had reported the possibility of a mine having been seen to be dropped in the river at that jetty. It was decided to move the vessel to the next one.

It was whilst the ship was being moved that she suddenly blew up. Not only was the ship engulfed in a fire ball, but a tug that was alongside was also destroyed, and a waterman's boat with two watermen, who were in the act of taking a mooring rope to one of the mooring dolphins, was also overwhelmed. The occurrence happened at about 4.30 p.m. I know this for a fact, as I was on the up-line platform of South Benfleet Station when the explosion occurred, while waiting for my train to Purfleet via Tilbury Riverside Station. We were always relieved at 5.30 p.m. on the *Redoubt* as this was the most suitable time to fit in with the train time tables.

The fire from that oil tanker was still burning for days, a grim reminder to river fraternity of what could happen. It was not very long after this that the *Redoubt* was required to take some loaded rubbish barges from the barge roads at Rainham, and place them alongside the Refuse Wharf for discharge. We were also to remove several of the empty craft and place them at the barge roads for collection by one of the London Tugs for onward delivery to the River Lee by way of Bow Creek. It may have been just chance that the craft that we moved were mainly old wooden-built canal barges or the fact that we had been 'wiped' in the last few days that possibly saved us from the fate of our sister tug the *Reserve* that was based and crewed from Erith on the Kent side of the river.

She hit a mine and was sunk just a half hour or so after we left Rainham in the very place that we had been working. Two of her crew were killed; the engineer and the boy mate. Some of these mines that were intended to fall into the river caused widespread casualties and damage ashore when they were dropped or fell in the wrong place. One in particular fell in the Borough of Lewisham where a school was hit, resulting in the death of over a hundred and seventy children with their teachers. These miss hits were classed as 'land mines', of which there were quite a few.

I have heard people who have survived some of these incidents say that they could hear the flapping of the parachutes to which the mines were attached long before they struck. On a lighter note, on one of the occasions when we were laying at Tilbury landing stage, waiting for our turn to be 'wiped', most of the crew adjourned to the fore cabin for a welcome cup of tea, leaving the skipper on his favourite perch, a high stool in the wheelhouse where he sat comfortably whilst at the wheel. Suddenly we felt a jolt that shook the tug violently causing us to heel over. Obviously we were on deck as soon as possible, if not quicker. The tug appeared at first glance to be settling by the stern.

With one accord most of us were on the pier and then we noticed that it was the tug's engines that were going astern thus giving the impression that the stern was lower in the water. The head rope was still secure and no one was in doubt that the skipper was in good voice in the wheelhouse. Looking along the pier, and very close to the walkway or brow where it sat on the pier, was a large hole with jagged edges protruding upward like a coronet. A bomb had gone through the pier and exploded beneath it. Fortunately there were no casualties except for the skipper's injured pride and a slight bruise on the engineer's bottom.

It became apparent that when the tug heeled with the force of the explosion, the skipper was thrown off balance as his stool tilted

Barge showing the result of bombing at Point Wharf, East Greenwich.

causing him to fall against the telegraph. The buckle of his waistcoat strap, looped itself over the telegraph handle causing it to ring down full astern.

The engineer George Stowers was also tilted off his perch in the engine room, but the fireman, Bill Freston, heard the ring on the telegraph and came through into the engine room from the stokehold, and seeing George on the floor apparently injured, obeyed the last order and put the engines astern. When all was quiet again and we were sure that the pier was not about to sink (it was built in separate watertight sections), we climbed back on board thinking, that was a bit too close for comfort.

On another occasion we had orders to run down to Mucking Flats, at the bottom of Lower Hope reach during one of our night shifts to take some loaded rubbish barges from the buoys where they were moored near the main channel and put them alongside the jetty where they were to be discharged, then bring any un-laden barges away. To complete this operation it was necessary to wait until just half an hour before high water or we would have insufficient water beneath the tug and tow to get alongside.

Just before midnight on a very dark night we began to move in over the mud-flats. Our eyes were accustomed to the dark so we knew where to head with our tow. At the very moment that we heard the approach of heavy aircraft, the wharf boatswain ashore decided to show a light indicating where he wanted the barges to be placed. As one, and at the top of our voices, we told him to put the so-and-so light out. He must have been deaf not to have heard us or the aircraft. 'What did you say?' he called.

Before we could repeat our very friendly advice, we heard the screech of the falling bombs. The first fell about two hundred yards away, the next about half that distance. I did not wait to see where the next one landed. I had jumped into the hold of the barge and was endeavouring to bury myself in the rubbish. Thankfully the last bomb fell some fifty yards away and only succeeded in giving some of us a mud bath.

Needless to say, the wharf boatswain was told that in future he was to put his torch where the sun could not shine, or we would definitely do the job for him. I, on the other hand, was not very welcome down in the fore cabin until I had removed my working gear and tied them to a heaving line and trailed them aft through the water to remove some of the smell from the rubbish. This was a useful way to clean our overalls so long as they were not forgotten. Those barges had been some three or four days in transit at the height of summer, so they were a little 'high' to say the least.

We all worked together fairly well as a team until young Bill Hardy volenteered for air crew training with the RAF. He was not kept long before he received his call up papers. I had tried to join the Navy, but was informed that I was in a reserved occupation; though I could volunteer for flying duties with the Air Force, somehow it did not appeal to me. I then tried the merchant navy but was informed that they were not taking first trippers.

Little did I know that my chance would come in the not too distant future. Bill Hardy's place in the crew was taken by a lighterman by the name of Bill Slater from Grays; he was about thirty-five years of age with some Seagoing experience and a very useful hand. He settled in well with the rest of the crew. In the meantime, my father was finding that his journey from South Benfleet to Woolwich Arsenal was getting to be too long-winded for him. So he decided on moving to a house in Ilford – this was not so far for him to travel, and could be done by using his bike alone. I did not mind as it meant that I had a shorter journey of just twenty minutes from Barking Station to Purfleet. It did mean, however, that I had to give up my Home Guard service.

One morning early in the spring of 1942, the *Redoubt* had orders to pick up four loaded rubbish barges from Cory's barge moorings, at East Tilbury, and tow them down to Mucking over the tide. We had been under way for about ten minutes or so when a blanket of fog enveloped us. We knew that a mine-spotting barge was moored in the vicinity – somewhere that we could take a temporary turn until the fog lifted. I could see the shape of a vessel approximately in the position where I expected the spotting barge to be, and told the skipper pointing in its general direction.

As we neared it, it started to move. We then realised that it was a Naval Patrol vessel that had gone onto the mud flat and was just freeing itself on the rising tide. The skipper put his helm over to bring us away from the mud when our screw was fouled by something un-yielding and we were held fast. Try as we might there was no way that we could clear the propeller; high water was passed and the ebb tide set in. Our tow consisting of four loaded rubbish barges swung down with the tide; our stern was held as though we had a kedge anchor streamed. After a couple of hours we were high and dry on the mud. We could then see that we had a thick submarine cable around the propeller shaft and that it would have to be cleared before we could get under way again.

Not having any means of communication onboard, we were wondering how we could let the company know of our predicament. Fortunately another of Cory's tugs came by who promised to pass the information on as soon as they could get ashore to telephone. Whilst we were pondering our next move we noticed a signal lamp flashing a morse code message to us from a signal hut on Coalhouse Fort – this was an old defense fort constructed to stop Napoleon from invading us.

There was also a similar fort at Cliffe Creek, and another at Tilbury. At first we wondered if they were signaling someone else.

Our foreman Joe Hardy had, as I previously mentioned, spent some time in the Inland Water Transport in the First World War, and fortunately he had retained a smattering of morse-code and semaphore knowledge, and was eventually able to inform the signal tower of our predicament regarding the cable. A message came back that we should try to remove it, but avoid cutting the cable if at all possible.

Bill and I stripped off to our underpants and lowered ourselves over the side. The mud was very thick, and we soon were up to our knees working in it. Some old gratings were brought over from the barges to be lowered over the stem for us to work from. It helped but still they became immersed in the mud.

Eventually we tied some lines to them to prevent them disappearing altogether; we managed to get one turn off by tying one of our towropes around the bight of the cable and using the anchor windlass on the bough of the nearest barge to haul it clear. It was hard work as only two men could put sufficient weight on the wooden spars that we were using to move the windlass barrel.

Eventually they broke under the strain. In the meantime we were running out of food, as we had been on duty from 5.30 p.m. the night before. We knew that we would incur some overtime but fully expected to be back at Purfleet by 7.00 a.m. at the latest, and yet here we were at midday and beginning to feel hungry as we had only brought sufficient food to last us twelve hours. What is more we had another six hours to look forward to before we could be relieved.

Joe explained our plight to the signal tower to see if they could assist. Three hours later when there was sufficient water around us to get alongside, a small boat from Cliffe Creek brought a loaf of bread and some runny butter. In the mean time Bill and I had managed to hack our way through the cable and buoy the ends. It was a matter of using about half a dozen hacksaw blades, an axe that just bounced off the cable at each stroke, and our knives that needed to be sharpened every five minutes.

We were certainly pleased to see our relief crew arrive in a spare tug to complete our tow; we had just twelve hours left before we started our next twelve-hour shift. I think that I fell asleep over my supper that evening. We did learn eventually that the cable that we

Tug and tow of six barges arriving in the upper Pool of London, *c.* 1952.

had fouled was a hush-hush installation that measured the magnetic field of ships using degaussing aparatus before they left the river.

We had been noticing for some time that trawlers had been seen leaving the Thames for destinations unknown towing lighters of about two hundred tons capacity in pairs. Obviously we were intrigued as to what purpose they were being put and why. I was soon to learn when I met one of my former tug skippers from my days with John Hawkins & Sons; George Doman. He was on Barking Station when I was on my way home one night. What is more he was in the uniform of a Petty Officer in the Royal Navy.

On speaking to him I learned that the barges were being converted into landing craft and that volunteers were being called for to man them. Furthermore he informed me that if I wanted to join I had better get down to Tilbury Dock and sign on. I was there the next day with young Jimmy Jewiss who now had his two years licence. We were signed on as Seamen SCO on a six-month contract that would pay us fifteen shillings a day. This was at least five times the amount that the average serviceman could expect. No wonder we were dubbed the millionaire mob.

Watermen, lightermen, dockers, and boatmen from all the major ports were invited to join. Tug skippers were automatically made Petty Officers, and lightermen acting mates were made 'leading Seamen'. In a little under a month I was told to report to Chatham Barracks. I became Seaman SCO, Number CJS948. I had joined the service that I dreamed of as a boy. I hadn't a clue what was in store for me, and the changes it would make to my future.

CHAPTER THREE

# THE MILLIONAIRE MOB

The day came when I received my calling up papers and was told to report to Chatham Barracks. This was on 8 June 1942 at 9.00 a.m., or to use naval parlance 0900. Arriving at the stated time I saw that I was amongst many well known members of the river fraternity including of course my old shipmate Jimmy Jewiss. Another chap, Bill Tewsley, a young freeman lighterman from Gravesend, was also amongst the twenty or so people reporting that morning.

I suppose that I ought to have considered myself lucky to be there, as about the same time that I had gone to Tilbury to volunteer, I had received my notice to go for a medical re-conscription for the Services. I did attend and passed all the tests with flying colours. I was then called in for an interview with an officer wearing the uniform of a major in the Army. 'Ah! Gaster,' he said, 'I understand that you put in a preference to go in the Navy. I'm sorry to have to tell you ...' Before he had the chance to say any more I said, 'Excuse me sir, would you please look at this,' and showed him the official piece of paper that I had been given at Tilbury stating that I was accepted for service in the Royal Navy. 'Well done,' he said. 'Good Luck,' he then shook my hand and I left. I breathed a sigh of relief as I preferred wearing bell-bottoms to wearing khaki.

Our joining day at Chatham commenced with a medical, though not too thorough, just enough to see that we had all the bits and pieces in the right places and that they were in reasonable working order. Then we were shepherded along to the clothing store to be issued with our kit. This consisted of uniform, steel helmet, oilskin sea boots, and service respirator, together with a hammock, two white blankets, and a small steaming bag. The normal kit bag being considered too big for the amount of clothing issued.

We were expected to purchase our own boots and other clothing. This caused a little consternation to our Petty Officer when we eventually managed to wriggle into our jumpers and bell bottoms, sometimes forgetting that the collar had to be fastened in position before pulling on the jumper. Then folding the silk to the correct dimensions and knotting it into place together with the white lanyard correctly placed under the collar and finished in front with the silk.

We were then supposedly ready for his inspection; we fell into line awaiting his critical eye and were rewarded with a shout of 'Brown boots!' They stood out like sore thumbs. The P.O. explained to the wearers of such footwear that unless they quickly obtained some black boots from the 'slops' or dyed their footwear black, they would never be allowed outside the barrack walls. He also pointed out to us that we had better get our clothing marked with our names as quickly as possible to prevent them going missing, as there were some light-fingered people in the barracks who would soon relieve you of any unattended clothing.

One of the Leading Seamen allocated to us showed us how to fold our jumpers inside out as well as our bell-bottom trousers, again inside out and in pleats that went across the leg in alternate folds, making seven creases in all. It was then advisable to find a couple of pieces of flat wooden slats of approximately ten inches by three inches to bind tightly round the creased and folded trousers to make the creases permanent. This was rather like a trouser press in miniature. The seven creases, we were told, represented the Seven Seas, the three white stripes on our collars or 'dickies' as the ladies were apt to call them, were supposedly there to represent Nelson's famous victories, and lastly, the black silk as a sign of mourning for that great man.

Our next learning process was in the art of preparing our hammock, tying the clews so that the hammock would easily open when climbing into it; again a wooden spreader at the head end would come in useful. Then there were the arrangements of the blankets, and finally slinging our hamnocks on to the hammock rails before getting into them and remaining there. This is not an easy task for the uninitiated, especially for some of our colleagues who were less sprightly – there were a few over forties amongst our ranks, but after a few struggles most of us made it.

After that came the most important lesson concerning hammocks: how to 'lash up and stow', which was the order given every morning. Your hammock had to be lashed with lashing supplied so that the blankets were rolled evenly in the length of the hammock, the canvas sides brought tightly round so that the blankets remained completely enclosed, then starting from the head end, which was sealed with a clove hitch, a series of half hitches, seven in a line which were passed around and along the body of the hammock, each pulled tight and finally secured at the foot end. The clews and the lashings were then secured along the length of the hammock to make a neat finish.

When a hammock was properly lashed in this manner it was supposed to support you in the water for several hours; fortunately I never had to test this theory. The lashed hammocks were then stowed in the hammock 'nettles'. This was a sort of pen with a wooden fence that the hammocks were stowed on end, so that they took up the least amount of room. I believe that in the days of wooden ships, they were placed to absorb any splintered pieces of wood flying about causing injuries to the crew during action.

We were also given more information about rank structure: who had to be saluted, who had to be obeyed, what various 'pipes' mean (pipes meaning the orders coming over the Tannoy following a boatswains call being sounded). We were told to salute the quarter deck when coming aboard and generally to act like a sailor.

I must say that we were probably treated a little different from the normal intake of recruits to the Navy, although we were still subject to Naval Discipline and the King's Rules and Regulations whilst we were in uniform. We were almost given the kid glove treatment for the whole time we were at Chatham. We had the usual foot drills and rifle practice, though the first time I took aim on the rifle range my shot was wide of the target. It was pointed out to me that the old Long Lee Enfield rifle that I was using had wing foresight guards and that I had aimed sighting on one of those. I realised that the Short Lee Enfield that I had been used to in the Home Guard had an aperture sight; I corrected my aim and scored a bull each time.

Before we leave the hammock drill too far, I should mention that after we had settled down in our hammocks on the first night, we were awakened by a din of a noisy and somewhat drunken crowd of 'Geordies' coming onto the mess-deck. These were the lads from Newcastle who had just arrived after a long and tiring journey.

Obviously they must have been in need of refreshment when they arrived in Chatham and so went to the nearest hostelry. It may have been that they were not used to the local brew. They tried several times to rig and get into their hammocks, finally giving up and sleeping on the deck where at least they did not have far to fall.

At the end of about three weeks in barracks we were entrained to Portsmouth where we shipped on board one of the old ferries and were conveyed to the Isle of Wight. For some of us it felt like going abroad.

On arrival at Ryde Pier, our bags and hammocks were loaded onto lorries whilst we were formed up into threes and marched to Puckpool on the north eastern point of the island where a holiday camp formally owned by Warner's had been taken over by the Navy and was now known as HMS *Medina*. It had been used prior to our arrival to train Fleet Air Arm personnel. I can imagine that we were something of a shock to the officers and staff of that establishment.

A meal had been arranged for us as soon as we arrived sometime after midday, then we were allocated our quarters which were in chalets around an open grass-covered area. There were two to a chalet so Jim and I had no problems sharing; we had been chums for some time, and had often stayed over at our respective homes. Bill Tewsley was sharing with some other person in the next chalet.

The following day we were given our station cards, which allocated our duty watch, and were put into parties of about twenty with one of our number allocated as class leader and made an unpaid Acting Leading Seaman. Our class leader was a chap called Sid Orde. He was a stevedore in civilian life working in the Royal Albert Docks. His choice was quite good as it turned out, he was aged about forty-five and a man of quiet manner who could get the lads to comply without having to shout or lose his temper.

We had training in weapon handling with Hotchkis and Lewis guns; these were the type that would normally be fitted to our craft. We were also given basic training in naval code flags so that we could operate in flotillas and try to 'keep station'. We practised sending morse code with torches, and were taught the art of semaphore. Our teachers had to be very patient people.

Finally we were introduced to our craft. Some were moored in nearby Wooton Creek. Our first introduction to the craft came as a bit of a shock. The modifications that had been made to convert them into landing barges left much to be desired. The wooden ceilings that had been the floor of the hold space had been ripped out and concrete poured in to replace them.

The concreting had been carried halfway up the sides of the hold between the stringers providing some reinforcement and protection for the hold space. A section of the after bulkhead and cabin area had been cut away by some ten feet across and approximately five feet above the floor of the hold. A platform extended aft from that point to the stern of the barge, and the sides of this cutaway area had been fitted with longitudinal bulkheads.

A ramp rose from the floor of the hold to the platform area, on either side of which a pair of Ford V8 engines fitted with vosper marine gear boxes were located. These were connected to a couple of shafts that extended through the after bulkhead of the hold, through the void that had been part of the cabin, to reappear on the outside of the after swim where propellers had been fitted. These were equi-distant on either side of the boarding ramp; the ramp was a heavy steel frame with a timber decking. There were hand winches fitted on either side of the boarding area with which to raise the ramp, an operation that required a lot of effort.

Between the inner and outer ramp, a couple of slotted brackets had been fitted to each longitudinal bulkhead. These were about fourteen inches apart and in them were placed heavy wooden planks that stretched across the opening, forming two temporary bulkheads. These were held secure by wooden wedges and were always to be left in place when the barge was under way or on passage.

Across the ramp area and above the temporary bulkheads was a slightly wider plank upon which the coxswain was expected to stand whilst manoeuvering the barge when under way; it was the only position that the stokers in control of the engines could see the hand signals given by the coxswain.

The coxswain was expected to stand facing the bows in plain view of the stokers, then, if he wanted to go ahead, move his arms forward; at forty five degrees meant half speed, fully extended meant full speed. By his side meant stop engines, moved backwards full astern. There were no half measures for astern movements. All very well if the engines were running at the same revolutions, there being no rudder to make any slight corrections to the course as the craft zigged and zagged as though on convoy evasive actions. As far as going astern, it was useless. The wash against the after swim defeated the thrust of the propellers.

With the ramp situated aft, which in these particular craft was the only option to keep them seaworthy, it was necessary to approach the beach going full speed ahead, probably all of four to six knots, depending on the shape of the barge (all varied depending where they were built) then swing into the wind or tide, whichever was strongest, by going ahead on one engine and astern in the other.

Then full speed astern on both engines, whilst at the same time dropping the bow anchor over the bow with which to help hold the crafts head to stop it swinging towards the beach, and, to help pull the barge away from the beach when required. In theory, it sounded quite simple – all one had to do then was to lower ramp, job done.

First and foremost communications between the coxswain and the stokers were not always easy. Should a sudden swell catch the barge and the coxswain move his arms in an endeavour to regain his balance on that rather narrow board, or perhaps decide to scratch his nose or other part of his anatomy, misunderstandings sometimes occurred leading to some rather colourful expressions from the man at the helm. More times than not a volunteer was pressed to swim or wade ashore with a light line to tie round a tree or other immovable obbject for the remaining crew on board to pull the barge ashore.

My main worry was that I was going to be the man on the plank when running the craft ashore, possibly on an enemy coast. I would not be protected from the weather let alone anything that the enemy might throw my way. It was obvious to me that the barges would need a lot of work to bring them up to a reasonably safe standard and suitable to carry out the work for which they were intended.

As it happens, I don't think that they were a complete waste of time. I am of the opinion that the spy planes sent over from Germany and France formed the opinion that we were ready to invade at any time after seeing all these barges moored in the many creeks and waterways of the south coast. So the German hierarchy turned a lot of their labour and workforces into building the West Wall.

Many of us were asked for our suggestions regarding the improvements to these barges, and I am pleased to say that they were listened to and acted on. However, that was to be some time in the future. In the meantime we settled down to boat training given by none other than Dod Osbourne a well known pre-war character who sailed an MFV around the Atlantic coast of Spain causing something of a furore in the national press at that time. The MFV was not his to take, according to press releases, and his navigation was supposedly done using a sixpenny atlas.

When he returned to England he was sentenced to a short term of imprisonment. His story, however, was that he was testing the durability of this type of vessel for the Admiralty for further use of these vessels under wartime conditions – well, he had done that trip whilst the Spanish Civil War was raging. I also know for a fact that he was later holding a commissioned rank in the Navy for which a conviction should have been an automatic bar.

We found his instruction most enlightening. His words were 'I can't teach you lads anything that you don't already know, so we'll go for tea and cakes at a friend of mine's bungalow on the seafront'. We all spent a lovely afternoon listening to his girl friend's gramophone whilst the whaler we were supposed to be training in sat on the beach.

One day we were informed that we were to be inspected by the Chief of Combined Operations, none other than Lord Louis Mountbatten. I was picked to be one of the Guard of Honour as I had gained a little more of the rifle drill whilst with the Home Guard. Other members of this guard were ex-First World War service personnel some with decorations earned in that previous war.

The Guard of Honour was drawn up on the lawn just inside the main gate when, shock and horror, it began to rain quite heavily. We stood there at ease waiting for the great man to appear, gradually getting wetter by the minute, the remainder of the SCOs drawn up behind us as in divisions. It was then noticed that a number of the officers were moving to the shelter of a glass canopy outside the regulating office.

A loud voice was heard from the ranks calling, 'You going to cover up?' The first lieutenant, a Lieutenant Commander, shouted, 'Silence,' then from the ranks came a resounding cry of 'Bollocks'. Perhaps I should mention that the cry, 'You going to cover up?' is widely used in the docks when the rain becomes too heavy to work in.

There ensued a deathly silence, and then the officers came from under the canopy making their way to the ranks. What had really upset the ranks was the fact that we had only one uniform each, which was getting wetter by the minute, leaving only our overalls to change into by way of dry clothing. It looked as though we might have to forgo our shore leave to dry out. At that precise moment, the main gate opened and in drove the Admiral to the shrill of the boatswain's pipes as he was piped aboard. As Lord Louis alighted from his car, his aide-de-camp held up his coat for him to put on.

Lord Louis took one look at us standing to attention in the rain and waved his coat away. Whether he had some insight as to what had gone on, or knowledge from above that the rain was about to stop, the miracle happened. The rain stopped and the sun shone. He inspected the Guard then called everyone to break ranks and gather round whilst he gave us a pep talk and a few well chosen jokes before departing to the wardroom. Nothing was ever mentioned again about the incident on the parade ground, or the near mutiny of 'The Millionaire Mob'.

Soon after this incident, about one hundred of us were transferred to Poole where our arrival caused something of a stir among the local population. Observing us marching up the road from the station, with our small steaming bags and naval issue hand cases that held our personal effects, and noticing the great difference in ages, they came to the conclusion that we must be survivors from a Russian Convoy. Some of the lads were quite happy to take advantage of the resultant hospitality showered upon them.

Our new quarters were to be in the Shaftsbury Homes on Constitution Hill, formally the home of young lads in need of care; well now they had some bigger lads to take their place. It was now a Naval Establishment under the name of HMS *Turtle*. Here we were to stay whilst learning all there was to know about being landing craft crews and coxswains – morse, semaphore and the flags pertaining to manoeuvres of the flotillas whilst underway.

We were encouraged to take part in exercises and sport which was entered into with enthusiasm. We had north versus south football matches, or should I say Newcastle versus West Ham? Some of the rules were not quite as per FA requirements, more like Australian rules and fifteen-aside rugby, but we had a lot of fun and made firm friends with our Geordie comrades.

It was not all fun and games. We were paraded into divisions every morning and allocated our tasks for the day by Chief Petty Officer Bun, a navy pensioner called back for the duration and known as Chiefy. I received my first promotion from Chiefy on my first day there: 'Lad,' he said. 'You will be Captain of the Heads for the week,' I thought to myself that he's alright, recognises talent when he sees it. Then I was told where to collect the necessary bucket, brushes, cloths and disinfectant from the Bosuns Stores: believe me when I say that it was a full time job that I was glad to see the end of.

The following week I stood in the back row, and succeeded only in being picked as galley assistant, which entailed mostly of peeling the spuds along with half a dozen others around a large galvanised tub. There must have been a hundred and fifty men not counting the officers to cater for, so there was plenty to do. The green vegetables were always prepared by the cook and his assistants to ensure that there was sufficient left to go into the pot.

After a few weeks, there were sufficient men under punishment and stoppage of leave to fulfill this task. Not that there were any serious misdemeanours, just the odd late returning on board after leave, or a case of too much imbibing whilst ashore. Although we were on board a 'stone frigate', as every shore establishment was termed, going out of the gate meant going ashore and not being aboard. We had the occasional route march to exercise our legs and minds, and to eye up the local talent. What's the saying, 'you're only young once'? If there were any dances going in the local Woodside Hall, they were well attended.

Bournemouth was not too far away, where a services club provided somewhere to spend a few hours and get a meal. Also there was the theatre where I saw my first operas, the *Barber of Saville* and, *La Traviata*, I was hooked on classical music from that day on. Quite often we, that is my shipmates Jimmy Jewiss, Bill Tewsley and I, would stretch our legs and walk the five or six miles back to our base.

Sometimes we would have afternoon tea above a large store that I think was called 'Bobby's' on a Sunday afternoon. I enjoyed that part of the world; it was a little different to the surroundings where I was brought up. I spent my nineteenth birthday on one of these jaunts; it must have been soon after our arrival at Poole.

It was about this time that I had a letter from my sister to say that she had not heard from her husband for some time. I knew that he was in DEMS Air, and had been for some time in charge of a catapult on a CAM Ship on convoy duties. A CAM ship was an ordinary cargo vessel, in his case the SS *Empire Tide*; she was fitted with a catapult that would launch a Hurricane fighter if attacked by enemy bombers. The pilot would have little chance if he was shot or forced down through lack of fuel unless an escort vessel was at hand, so they were only used as a last resort.

We did not know exactly where he was, but thought that he might be on one of the Russian runs. Soon after this I received a telegram to say that she had heard from him to say that he was on his way home, and could I get leave for the occasion. I went to see my Divisional Officer and explained that Alf was like a brother to me as I had none of my own, and was granted a long weekend from that Friday.

When I got home I learned that Alf had been on the ill-fated PQ17 convoy where they were told to scatter because of the fear of the German battle cruisers being out in the Norwegian fiords. We all know that this was the case, due to the loss of so many ships. They had to head north up into the ice and make the best way they could. Eventually they made Murmansk where the reception they had was anything but friendly, and then on to Archangel.

I'm not sure of the true figure of ships arriving; I think that it was something like eleven cargo vessels in all. Once they had discharged their cargos and managed to refuel their bunkers and taken in fresh water and some supplies (this took them some time) they were joined by another six vessels making seventeen in all for the return run home. Three of these eventually made it back to the Clyde.

We celebrated his safe return. He had with him a shipmate who was a steward. I joined them at the bar – after all I was a sailor and could not let the side down! However it was not long before my legs let me down. I was fine until we left the pub, The Rose and Crown on Ilford High Street, and entered the alleyway that went through to

Uphall Road leading to my home. It was there that my legs went to rubber causing me to lose control of them.

Fortunately I had my father and brother-in-law on either side to keep my equilibrium, although I don't think I could have said that word to save my life at that time. But I 'knew' that I was 'sober', it was just my legs that were the culprits. Perhaps it was all those whiskeys and chasers that we had managed to down. Yet it did not seem to have the same effect on my brother-in-law and his shipmate. I think that I had learned just what it meant to be legless and was very carefull not to get that way again.

On returning to Poole I was asked by one of our officers, a Lt Bishop RNR, if I was interested in learning coastal navigation. If so he would be willing to teach any of us who were interested. I was more than interested, and together with a few more of the lads, he started some evening classes in one of the many school rooms on site. He advised us on our next long weekend leave to acquire a book of Norries Nautical Tables, and a copy of Tate's Home Trade Guide from a maritime dealer situated in Fenchurch Street. I knew the place well, having haunted that area in my school days.

From then on I was captivated in learning the art of navigation. I had wanted to go to the George Street School of Navigation in Poplar, but was unfortunate in there not being sufficient scholarship places when I sat my exams. My parents thought that I would have earned more money as a compositor in the print trade. Believe me when I say that at that time my literary skills were not great. As a compositor, I would have been useless.

Lieutenant Bishop gave us a good grounding in the art of chartwork. He taught us the meaning of variation and deviation and the effects they have on a compass course. He also showed us how to work out the tides from the phases of the moon using the High Water Full and Change as shown on the charts.

As we progressed under his tuition, we learned how to work out our longitude by chronometer and finally our latitude by meridianal altitudes. A few of the lads dropped out, but this was something new to me, I was now in a world of logarithms, as long as I had the formula it sorted itself out for me.

He then got us out of the classroom into a harbour launch that we collected from Beaulieu and brought round to Poole Harbour, even testing my skills on the Aldis Lamp, when challenged by a guard vessel as we emerged from the Solent.

A few months later when we were nearing the end of our six months contractual period, we were all asked whether we wanted to stay on in Combined Operations, or would we prefer to return to 'Civvy Street'. If we stayed on, we would revert to ordinary naval rates of pay, but we had a good chance of promotion.

A number of the SCOs chose to leave, including Bill Tewsley; I understand that he decided to go into the Rescue Tugs Service, of which I knew little at that time. Jim and I decided to stay on. We were given a test in seamanship, boat-handling, rope work, morse and semaphore signalling.

We must have passed, for just a few weeks later we were informed that we would be going to Chatham where we would both be up-rated to Petty Officer Coxswain. It was January before we left for Chatham, prior to that we had a wonderful Christmas at Poole. The lads put on a 'Sods Opera' that was attended by all the officers and their wives, who were very surprised when 'rounds' was sounded, and in marched 'Adolf', 'Benito' and 'Hiro Hito', goose-stepping their way around the hall.

I must say that the CO took it really well and laughed more than most. The famous three lads who instigated this charade were well known for their practical jokes, having worked together in the Regents Canal Dock in Stepney.

On the 21 January 1943, after a thorough medical examination in Chatham Barracks, I was enlisted for a period until the end of the present emergency, as an A.B. On 22 January as a Leading Seaman and on the 23rd, as a Petty Officer. I understand that the reason for the one day in each of the ranks of A.B. and Leading Seaman, was in case I was found wanting in the rank of Petty Officer, there was always a rank that I could be busted to. My pay at that time was seven shillings and sixpence a day, half of what I was previously getting as a Seaman SCO.

I was happy to say that at last I collected my full issue of clothing from the store: shirt and ties, uniforms two of blues, two of whites; in fact I had a full kit bag to carry around. We had to report to the east camp in Chatham Barracks for our accomodation. Then to the Petty Officers mess where I had to see the 'President of the mess'. He was a grey-haired three-badge man, meaning that he had many years' service. 'Right lad,' he said. 'Give me your rank, name, religion, and T or G.' I gave my name, told him I was C. of E., and told him I was UA.

'T' meant that I was Temperate and did not take my rum issue for which I would then be entitled to three pence a day in lieu. 'G' meant that I would be entitled to my rum issue or grog (this is a mixture of rum and water), though in the case of Petty Officers, that would be neat, and UA meant that I was under age. His face suddenly changed to a shade of purple he stood up and threw his cap that had been on the desk onto the deck, he then executed a little dance on it.

'Cor blimey, they'll be making up bloomin babies next,' he spluttered. It had probably taken him the best part of twelve years to make the rank, and there was I, nineteen years and five months with just three months service behind me, holding the same rank. I felt slightly embarrassed, though I believed that I had the necessary experience to do the job that I was picked for.

We only spent a few days at Chatham, during which time I was able to get home for a few hours to see my family in Ilford and have a few 'jars' with my father in the local. They were surprised to see me in my new rig, although by the time I got home the white collar on my new shirt was almost blue from the dye of my jacket. It was some time before this rectified itself, so I was forever 'dying' my shirts to keep them white. I explained to them that I had been promoted to petty officer coxswain in Combined Operations, and my new official number was C/JS 332916, the C/JS showing me as a Chatham rating, later to be changed to P/JS when I was transferred to Portsmouth.

On returning to Poole, we found that at least three quarters of the SCO lads had opted out and had returned to 'Civvy Street', many of them to be called up for service in the Inland Water Service of the Royal Engineers. We, on the other hand, were all Petty Officers with exception of one chap by the name of Learmouth who had chosen to be an A/B Seaman. At first we wondered why until we learned that he had eleven children and that put him on the same pay scale as a Lieutenant Commander with all his service family allowances. I still found this hard to believe. He enjoyed staying on to become the P.O.'s mess-man during the remainder of our time there.

Again we had further instruction in the art of navigation and signals together with some foot drill from the Chief Petty Officer.

Whilst there we learnt that another visit was being made by our Chief of Combined Operations, Lord Louis Mountbatten. This time we were ready, a smartly turned out guard of Petty Officer Coxswains, who were complemented for their effort and wished success in their forthcoming role. A few more quips and then the Salvation Army tea wagon arrived as we were dismissed. What a debt we owe to those people who looked after the forces and their families during the war.

I was able to purchase for myself a doeskin suit of number ones for my ventures ashore and looked very smart with the gold wire badges denoting my rank together with the Combined Operations Badge on the sleeve. Although I did have trouble convincing a black labrador dog who had adopted us and spent many hours in the sentry box with us when we were doing our night duty on the main gate. He would tolerate anyone in bell-bottoms, but drew the line at officers and petty officers who tried to pet him.

I had spent many hours on that gate with him curled up in the sentry box behind me. He would appear to be asleep, then his ears would prick up and a little growl would bring you to alert. He would sense that someone was approaching long before they became audible to whoever was on sentry duty.

On my first day back at Poole in my new rig, 'Turtle' as we had called him was just inside the gate adjacent to the sentry box. 'Hello Turtle,' I said as I reached out fondle his ears as per normal, I quickly changed my mind as he showed me his teeth and gums. As far as he was concerned, I was on the other side. An intake of seamen and stokers arrived to take over our old mess decks. These were the new crews who we would have to train to man the landing barges that were being modified in various parts of the country.

Some of my time was now taken up exercising them with route marches, and having to sort out the 'chaff' from the 'wheat'. We had a few 'skates' amongst them who tried it on to see what they could get away with. I left them in no doubt that I could deal with them if I had to. Mostly they were a pretty good bunch who would sort out the awkward ones amongst themselves.

Within a few weeks, about a dozen of us coxswains were moved down onto Round Island situated in Poole Harbour. It was a wonderful location. The island previously belonged to a very wealthy gentleman who had his own boatman and gardener living in purpose-built houses on the island. This is where we found ourselves quartered. The main house situated on the east side of the island had a magnificent view of Poole and Sandbanks from the principal bedroom; this had mirrors set in the walls at a level so that if you were seated or lying down, a panoramic view of the harbour was there to be seen.

This was the classroom where the coxswains were brought up to date with chart work and navigation studies. The remainder of the house was the officers' quarters and wardroom. Soon after arriving on the island, I met our new CO Lt Russel-Smith, an ex tug master employed by Tilbury Dredging and Contracting Company on the Thames. I was put in charge of a salvage team that had the job of re-floating some of the mark one LBV's that were sunk at their moorings around the island. This was not such an awkward job as it would appear; Poole Harbour experienced four tides a day as did a number of the coastal resorts along that stretch of the English Channel between Weymouth and the Solent. The tidal range was therefore much less than that on the Thames and other rivers.

At low water the coamings and gunwhales of the water-logged barges were above the surface. So by plugging the pump boxes, using tarpaulins to reinforce the temporary bulkheads, and using as many pumps, both motor and hand shifting them in unison, we were able to bring the barges up to a level where the ramp opening was above the external water level. It meant 'all hands to the pumps', for an hour or so, and then a good cleaning session to rid the barge of the accumulated mud in the cabin and hold spaces.

There were about four or five of these craft in all to be re-floated in this manner; however, another barge that had sunk in deeper water in the main channel had to be tackled differently. I was lucky to be able to call on the services of the very same tug-skipper that I worked with when I first started my apprenticeship on the Thames, George Doman. He was the person that I had met at Barking Station who had informed me about the Millionaire Mob. George was then in command of a tug called the *Primate* which had been commandeered from Palmers Towage Company on the Isle of Dogs back on the Thames. There were several of the smaller tugs from the Thames which had been acquisitioned for the purpose of moving the craft around.

With the assistance of an engineer officer who was commanding one of the first landing barges that had been modified and converted by LBE, Landing Barge Engineering, we were able to splice a number of five-inch wire strops, allowing them to pass under the sunken barge, using the tug to coax them into place. Then with four LBVs on either side lying with the forward swims over the sunken barge, and a further two on at the bow and one over the stern, the strops were taken in tight at low water and then it was a matter of waiting until the tide did its work and hoping that the bitts to which the wire was fastened would hold the weight.

As the tide rose, the forward swims of the craft were pulled lower in the water, the stern lifting so that the screws and fixed budgets cleared the water. We held our breath and waited. The sunken barge did lift sufficiently for the *Primate* to push the lifting craft and their burden out of the fairway into shallow water. The operation was continued on the next tide, the strops having been readjusted and any slack taken in. Then, as before, came the clearing up operation.

Our next job was returning a barge that had been broken adrift from her moorings and driven up onto the beach on a spring tide during a gale. This was tackled by tunnelling beneath her, then placing large 14-inch piles under her so as to protrude on either side, and then large hydraulic jacks were used to allow wooden rollers to be put into position along the length of the barge. The following day at high water, the *Primate* and another little Thames tug, the *Tommy Lea* of Thames Steam Tug & Lighterage Co., working in tandem, pulled the lighter back into deep water.

I was fortunate that most of these operations were carried out in a warm and sunny May, for I was working in my shallow diving gear, a pair of ordinary swimming trunks as I positioned the strops etc., thankful that we were on the South Coast and not the distant North.

It was about this time that I was approached by Lt Bishop RNR, He told me that he was being transferred to HMS *Manatee* on the Isle of Wight, and that he wanted me to take over the Navigation classes on Round Island. I was stunned and said that I had no sea time in and it would not be the blind leading the blind. He told me not to worry, and that I would have to make sure that I could answer any awkward questions by making sure of my answers, that way I would learn all the quicker, and in any case I was good enough.

His parting shot really threw me: 'By the way, you are now a CW candidate.' 'What does that mean?' I asked. 'I have put you down for a commission with the approval of Lt Russel-Smith,' he replied. 'I am not sure that I want a commission,' I replied. 'I don't want to be a mid-shipman'. He looked a little taken aback and asked how old I was. When I told him he said, 'I understand that the age for Sub-Lieutenant is now being lowered to nineteen and six months,' and also that it would be a few months before I would be going to take the necessary exams. I said that I was quite happy within the flotilla and that I would miss all my shipmates. His answer was that I would always 'have friends wherever you go; don't miss this opportunity'.

I did have the opportunity of taking a modified LBV on trials, bringing her away from the yard where she had been converted. She now sported a wheel-box on the starboard quarter alongside the ramp opening; this had some armour shielding around it giving some protection to the coxswain. Also, it was fitted with a bell system for communication with the stokers. No more arm movements on a narrow plank that could be misinterpreted. The new and more powerful engines were Gray's Royal Marine petrol units. A rudder had been fitted under the starboard quarter that gave very limited steerage; a small fixed budget still remained under the starboard quarter.

This nearly proved disastrous as we sailed through Hamworthy Bridge; the LBV took a turn to starboard toward some light wooden built personnel landing craft. Even with the rudder hard over to starboard it had little effect. I had to put the starboard engine astern before she answered the helm. I could imagine what a two hundred ton barge would have made of those little craft against that quay wall.

The mark two LBV's had a few variations, some as I previously mentioned had been converted into Engineering LBVs, others for fuelling LBOs, water carriers LBWs, ack ack, LBFs, and perhaps the most welcome on the beaches floating feeding stations, Landing Barge Kitchen LBKs.

I went on leave shortly after this and my family and friends, on seeing me, thought that I had been in the Mediterranean area. I was as brown as a berry, and as fit as the proverbial fiddle. The following weekend, I went to the open air swimming baths in Barking Park and

LBK in action, providing hot meals.

enjoyed some admiring glances from a few of the young ladies who were there – Oh to be young again!

As I was leaving the park entrance in Ilford Lane, I met my former friend and workmate from my days and nights on board the *Redoubt*, Bill Hardy, dressed in a RAF Sergeant Pilot's uniform and looking very smart. We spoke for just a minute or two. He explained that he had to catch his train back to Purfleet; it was due to leave very soon. However, he did have enough time to tell me that he was flying 'Mosquitos'. We agreed that the next time we had a get together, that a tot would be taken. Sadly, Bill was reported missing, believed killed, soon afterwards. He was never found.

On returning to Round Island after a very enjoyable leave, I was invited up to the wardroom back at HMS *Turtle* for the evening together with a couple more lads who had been made C/W candidates. We were made very welcome in a very friendly atmosphere that did not lack a few drinks to make us feel at home. We were given a very friendly talk as to what was expected when we arrived at the officer training establishment in Scotland for Combined Operation Naval Officers, HMS *Loch Ailort*, for a six-week intensive course that included navigation, signals, pilotage, and boat handling, to name just a few.

We were expected to undergo plenty of physical training including assault courses and running practically every day, on top of which we would have to last at least three one-minute rounds in a boxing ring. All this would be under the scrutiny of a very critical staff looking for any failing that would eliminate your chances of a Commission.

I was lucky in that I had two cousins who were amateur boxers with whom I had sparred on numerous occasions, and furthermore that a chap by the name of Stan Everard, who had run a weight training club before he joined, was on the island with us and agreed to give me some boxing lessons, together with some general training to get me in shape.

Stan took me under his wing, we set up some parallel bars with some odd bits of piping found on the island, acquired some boxing gloves from the stores and set to work getting me fit and ready for Loch Ailort. Every weekend we would go ashore at Arne, an adjacent little village that had been evacuated of its civilian population to be taken over by the Army for training purposes, then walk from there to Corfe Castle, a distance of some ten miles, to have a meal. We would then walk all the way round Poole Harbour to Parkstone, via Wareham, a distance of twenty-odd miles accompanied by Jimmy Jewiss who was stationed on the island with us. We had a bit of excitement one day when the army lads were doing their usual tank training exercises with live rounds, some of which landed on the southern edge of the island. It took some time before we were able to contact them with a few frantic telephone calls and succeed in getting the shelling stopped.

The day came when I eventually said goodbye to my friends on the island and to the landing barges. I was off to Scotland via Portsmouth Barracks. I only spent one night there, but not before a farewell drink was taken in the wardroom of HMS *Turtle* and I was wished good luck by the officers there.

The overnight journey up to Glasgow, where we arrived bleary eyed the next morning, was very uncomfortable in a well packed train, so the apperance of a tea wagon manned by the Salvation Army was a welcome sight. The tea and rolls went down well.

# CHAPTER FOUR

# LOCH AILORT

We were soon on our way from Glasgow to Inveraray where we found ourselves accommodated on what looked like a Mississippi steamboat. There were two of these vessels there, The *Northland* and the *Southland* manned by merchant navy personnel and flying the Red Ensign. They were ideal accommodation vessels with plenty of cabins, though a little on the small side. The next day we had an interview ashore with a Commander RN. He saw us individually and had a word with us to see if we felt that we would feel at home in the wardroom. I said that I had many friends who were officers and I had not felt uncomfortable with them. He wished us good luck on the commissioning course and for the future.

We were then introduced to the establishment at Inveraray, HMS *Quebec*, where we would go before going to Loch Ailort. This time was not wasted, as we were introduced to an assault course where the instructors seemed to take a great delight in firing their fixed, or so they said, Lewis guns over our heads whilst we were traversing a bog up to our necks in very muddy slime with our rifles held above our heads, forcing us to duck into the gooey mess. If we got our rifles contaminated with the slightest bit of this muck, it was a case of cleaning them and starting over again. Eventually we satisfied their seemingly sadistic pleasures and finally emerged looking like walking mud-covered mummies whose boots squelched green slime with every foot step.

Another time we spent a whole day on the firing ranges, with both rifle and revolver, firing at targets that popped up from unexpected places, each time with a double shot. We felt happy about that until we were informed that some of the targets were friendly. Eventually the day came when we proceeded to Loch Ailort where we were issued with a white band that we had to put round our caps, and were told that henceforth we were to be known and addressed as cadet rating, regardless of any rank that we had previously held. Furthermore, we were to conduct ourselves properly at all times and should be correctly dressed in the rig of the day as required, with oilskins folded neatly and buttons showing when carried over the left forearm.

We wondered why the special note had been given about the oilskins. It soon became obvious that rain was also the order of the day; for the whole six weeks that I spent at Loch Ailort, it failed to rain on three days only. When it was not raining we were under constant attack from swarms of midges; these little devils seemed to take a delight in attacking us when we were drawn up on parade where we were forced to stand to attention without moving a muscle or allowing a twitch to show.

The instructor would take a delight in growling, 'Keep your face straight laddie.' We just had to grin and bear it. That first week showed us what to expect for the remainder of the six weeks that we were to be at Loch Ailort. At 0630 it was up and into our shorts, vest, and gym shoes then out onto the parade ground for some rigorous exercises for half an hour, then back to our quarters for a quick change into the rig of the day for breakfast. Then on parade in divisions for 0800. From then until 1200, apart for a short stand easy, we would be into instruction classes for the whole of the forenoon. Then from 1200 it was lunch until 1300, resuming instruction classes until 1600.

It was then a race to our quarters to quickly change into P.T. gear again then fall in on the parade ground once more ready for our last exercise of the day as follows. In the first week it was a run round the inner circle, a distance of approximately one mile, in the shortest possible time. Each one of us was aware that we were under constant surveillance with notes being made on our performances. The following week it was the outer circle, a distance of one and a half miles. Week three, entailed both circuits, whilst week four entailed the inner, outer and the assault course. By this time you were either fit or completely knackered, and anyone seen not to be giving his best was dismissed from the course and sent back to his division. On the fifth week, doing endurance tests required one to climb a nearby mountain then return to the parade ground in the shortest possible time.

It was no use turning round halfway; you had to collect a card from a P.T.I. who had climbed up during the afternoon. I believe that the record time in reaching him was something like twenty-five minutes. My time was more like thirty-five to forty minutes though I did make up for this on the way down when I slid for what felt like a hundred yards on my posterior ending up in a bog at the bottom. This saved my neck, or should I say my bottom from further punishment.

During the latter part of this week we were all required to go into the boxing ring against an opponent picked of equal weight from the preceding division. The chap that I found myself matched against was taller by some three inches with a corresponding reach. I feared the worst.

Fortunately I had that little bit of experience from sparring with my cousins, plus the extra training that Stan Everard had given back on Round Island. On the night of the fights I found myself third on the bill. I was somewhat put off when the first of my colleagues was soundly beaten and the second knocked out in the first round. I climbed into the ring prepared for the worst. When the bell rang and we met in the center of the ring and touched gloves, I instinctively kept my guard up and led out with my left into the face of my adversary contacting him hard on his nose. Immediately there was blood everywhere and it seemed to take all the go out of him. From then on I felt good, though I was more than pleased to hear the final bell at the end of those three one minute rounds. I never realised just how long those three minutes could seem when your legs felt like lead and every movement was an effort. The fact that I won was more by luck than expertise, though I felt good.

The fifth week was also taken up with examinations in all requirements of the course. Chart work, seamanship, signals, pilotage, P.T., and field training. The course was comprised of all the requirements of the General Service Branch with the addition of the endurance and assault course training to bring us up to the standard required by Lord Louis Mountbatten, who believed that no officer should give an order that he could not carry out himself.

The sixth and last week was a little more relaxing. We had some time to go sailing on the loch in whalers. This I thoroughly enjoyed though I was a little concerned with regard to my results. I had not made a good start on my chart-work paper due to overeagerness at the beginning. I had written down the wrong course to steer, only to realise my mistake a little way through the paper. I managed to rectify it but left myself little time to finish. Then came the fateful day, when we were to learn our destiny: promotion, or return to the ranks. We had been told that some of us were to be interviewed by the examining board, so it was no surprise to me when my name was called. I was instructed that upon entering the room, I was to turn left and advance to a spot marked on the deck facing a desk and there to announce my name and rank to the board that was sitting.

I entered as directed and found myself facing more gold braid than I had seen since joining the Navy. The senior officer, a captain who I later learned was in command of the Western Approaches, asked me to explain why I had failed to complete my chart-work in the exam question. He informed me that I had pass marks but could not understand after doing so well in chart-work all through the course why I had not completed the paper.

I explained through exam nerves I had misread the course given at the start of the paper and that it was not until I had laid out my first fix that I realised my mistake. Although I had restarted the paper I had insufficient time left to complete. He asked me whether I would be willing to take another test and I said, 'Gladly, Sir.' He turned to the senior instructor, a commander, and asked him to arrange the test right away.

I was led to an upper room where I was given a new set of questions to tackle. After some fifteen minutes I was told that I had done sufficient work. The commander had a quick check of the work and without letting me know how I had coped, bade me follow him down to the room where the board was sitting. He knocked and entered; it seemed ages that I was waiting outside that door. I had visions of them going over my work with a magnifying glass and shaking their heads. All the other cadets had long left the building, I was on my own.

Eventually the door opened and my name was called; 'Come in Gaster.' I entered the room and carried out the same procedure, advanced up to the desk and was about to announce my name when I realised that no one was sitting behind it. I then realised that the examining board had moved and were now propping up the mantelpiece drinking cups of tea. I turned to face them. The Captain spoke first. 'Yes, you have passed, why couldn't you have done that the first time? What would have happened if you had made that mistake aboard your tug back on the Thames?' I replied that we only did lamppost sailing on the Thames. 'Whatever is that?' he asked. So I told him that we were never out of sight of land and knew every light on the river. He laughed and said I could go. I thanked him and made my way back to my colleagues. I think that I was walking on air, almost missing the ship's postman who handed me a telegram. On opening it I read the one word 'congratulations'; it was from my parents.

They were curious when they had to write 'cadet rating Gaster' on letters addressed to me at Loch Ailort, so I had to explain that I was on a commission course, and that if I was still there on the sixteenth of September then I would pass. Little did they know the sweat that I had shed those last few hours. I was sorry to say that my three colleagues who had left Poole with me failed to finish the course. But I had met two other lads from the Thames who were coxswains from the LBVs and who, like me, had made it.

That afternoon we were paraded and handed our Commissions by the captain. When it came to my turn, he shook my hand and asked, 'Feeling better now Lad?' I assured him that I was. That evening we were all invited to the wardroom for tea and light refreshments – we were also given our postings. All of the sixty odd ratings who had been newly commissioned were posted to landing craft as First Lieutenants with exception of six, myself included, who were required to report to HMS *Armadillo* at Ardentinny for Royal Naval Beach Commando Training.

My new role was to be that of an Assistant Beach Master. However first I was to take fourteen days leave during which time I was to purchase my new uniform, that of a Sub-Lieutenant RNVR and report back to Inveraray for landing craft familiarisation. I often wondered what made me Commando material. Was it the boxing or the poor chart work exam result? Either way I was never going to find out so I just accepted the fact that I was going to do my best whatever I was called upon to do.

We had a slight hangover the next morning after letting our hair down in the canteen the night before. After abstaining from drink for the best part of six weeks, we celebrated. We, being Joe Smith and Laurie Francis, my ex-landing craft colleagues who were previously based on the Isle of Wight, made our way into Glasgow the next morning. There at Rowans, the big naval outfitters, we spent some of the fifty five pounds uniform allowance, purchasing a smart new uniform together with shirts and collars, ties, shoes and raincoat etc. so that we could travel home looking more like tailor's dummies. It seemed strange to be on the receiving end of salutes and we were a little self conscious in our new roles.

Joe and Laurie lived fairly close to my home in Ilford, one in East Ham and the other in Plaistow both in East London. We spent a few days of our leave together but soon lost track when they went to join there respective landing craft, whereas I was destined to spend the next fifteen months more as a soldier than a sailor. It was an experience that I was to remember for the rest of my life and never once regretted.

My leave went all too quickly; my parents wanted me to visit aunties and uncles that we had not seen for years, wanting to show me off. On one such occasion after returning from Pitsea by train to Barking Station, a woman wanted to know what time a certain train was due, I said sorry madam I don't know. Well you ought to know she said, thinking I was a railway guard.

My mother who was with me at the time was most indignant though had a good laugh afterwards. On returning to Scotland, and Inveraray in particular, I was again accommodated on the *Southland* with the six newly promoted officers destined to become Naval Commandos but first we had games to play, that is, war games in mock landings with the army lads and the use of live ammunition, so this was not the place to make mistakes.

It was very demanding during the dark hours, trying to follow in the wake of craft ahead of you onto an unknown beach where the only illumination was from tracer bullets flying over your heads, thunder flashes and gun-cotton charges exploding on the beaches in

Jack as a Sub-Lieutenant.

the landing area. Someone thought fit to cheer us up by saying that we were allowed twenty percent casualties during training. I had the strange feeling that the person responsible for organising these fun and games was trying to hit this target.

We were at Inveraray for something like a month during which time I was acting Provost Marshal in the town. I did not mind that duty as a supper was laid on at a nice little tavern and very little trouble came from the lads on shore leave. I enjoyed being able to handle all the various types of landing craft all of which were far easier to manoeuver than our old LBVs.

The day eventually arrived when we packed our bags and baggage and said goodbye to the Southland and piled onto a three-ton lorry and headed for Ardentiny, the home of the Royal Naval Commando Training Establishment, HMS *Armadillo*. Whatever we had done before could no way compare with what we were about to experience. Life was never going to be quite the same again. Were we up to it? We were soon going to find out.

At the end of a pleasant ride through the Scottish countryside, we arrived at a lovely old house set in pleasant surroundings overlooking Loch Long. Here we were met by a smart looking RN Lieutenant dressed in a khaki battle dress with Combined Operation badges on the top of each sleeve and the letters RN COMMANDO above them.

'Allow me to introduce myse,lf' he said. 'I am Lt Wake, your training officer. The time is now 1200. I want you to go away and have your lunch then be back here in your oldest rig at 1300 sharp.'

CHAPTER FIVE

# ARMADILLO

It seemed strange when we entered the wardroom to see so many khaki uniforms, especially when they were being worn by naval officers. We hurried over our meal in order that we could change and be ready for whatever was in store for us that afternoon. At the appointed hour we fell in, not wishing to put ourselves in the bad books on our first day, and on the stroke of one, our training officer appeared; with a quick 'follow me' he was halfway down the drive leading to the road at a fair trot. We took off after him not wishing to be left behind and soon found ourselves running along the same road that we had traversed when arriving from Inveraray, the question 'had we been found wanting?' and 'are being returned as rejects?' crossed my mind. We carried on at a lively pace and I was beginning to enjoy it; this cross-country was fine. Suddenly we darted through a gap in the hedgerow and began to continue to run up the side of a mountain.

I was beginning to regret eating quite so much lunch. The six weeks since we had any steady training at Loch Ailort was also beginning to take its toll; we had gone soft. Arriving at a point about halfway up the rise, Lt Wake called out for us to rest. Most of us immediately sank to the soft mossy turf under our feet. I am sure that only a minute could have elapsed when again came the call 'follow me'. We dragged ourselves to our feet and once more entered the chase after our leader, on and on and upward we climbed, for now it was getting steeper with every step and the pace did not slacken. I could sense that we were nearly at the top and I was looking forward to the inevitable break that surely must be waiting for us at the summit. We dragged ourselves those last few paces that put us on top of the mountain finding ourselves too exhausted to enjoy the wonderful view.

As we sank to the moss at the order to rest, we thought, 'it's all down hill from here', blissfully unaware of what further delights were in store for us before reaching our accommodation once more to enjoy a nice cup of tea. With these thoughts going through my mind I was suddenly brought back to reality with the words 'follow me'. I am sure that we had only just sat down. Running in his wake, we set off on the way down. I am sure that he must have been chuckling to himself as we started to follow the course of a stream, not alongside it, but in it. It became deeper and faster flowing as we progressed; here and there were small waterfalls formed by the stream passing over outcrops of granite. These were negotiated fairly easily at first; however we found that they grew steadily bigger the more we progressed downstream. In some places where the steady flow of water had carved through the rock, it became necessary for us to brace our feet against one wall with our shoulders against the other as we eased ourselves down the slippery walls of the watercourse.

I cannot remember stopping on the way down. Time seemed to stand still and the afternoon seemed endless. Eventually we arrived on the roadway bordering the Loch at a distance of about a mile from the camp. We collected and then proceeded at a trot along the road to our eventual destination.

At a point some two hundred yards from the gates we came to a halt. 'Right lads, into the Loch and swim over to the pier, then you can go and get yourselves a hot bath and change for tea.' How I or anyone else made it I do not know, we crawled back to our quarters soaked to the skin and though it was the first week in November, I don't think any one uf us were aware of the cold. We were too exhausted to notice. That evening, after we had changed, we had to parade in one of the training huts where Lt Wake gave us his introduction talk with a promise that we could look forward to more of the same in the weeks to come.

He firstly impressed on us the importance of being able to carry out any order that we would be required to give and therefore would expect the best from us during the training period. He also told us that we would be issued with two suits of khaki and two suits of denims the next day. 'You will be expected to parade in khaki for 'colours' in the mornings and to remain in that rig for training periods except where the assault course or beach landings are involved. On those occasions you will wear denims; these are easily dried in the large drying room provided where no doubt yesterday's rig was to be found.

'Luncheon and tea will be taken in your khaki uniform, but dinner will always be attended in blues, there will be no exception to this rule even though you may be taking part in night exercises later. You will find that ample time will given for you to change for these exercises, you will not, repeat will not, wear your khaki for shore leave or home leave.' During those following weeks it seemed that all our time was taken up in changing from one wet rig into a fresh dry one, only to change back into blues for dinner, then back into denims for night landing exercises, returning to the little kitchen at the back of the wardroom in the early hours of the morning for a hot cup of thick 'Kai', as the cocoa was called, before climbing up to the drying room to exchange our wet clothing ready for the next days hard training, from there it was into a hot bath before crawling into bed to sleep the sleep of the exhausted.

We were soon initiated into the secrets of the assault course with its death-slide – this spanned the river going from the top branches of a tree on one side, to the base of a tree on the other bank around which were thick gorse bushes. This was traversed by using our toggle rope, an item that we were all supplied with. These ropes were about a fathom in length with an eye splice in one end, and a stout wooden toggle in the other. By joining the toggle and eye splice together, this when passed over the death slide, would form two loops and passed under each elbow would make a safe sling with which to descend at a rate of 'knots'. Here, on arrival at the base of the tree, it was necessary to raise the feet to prevent contact with the tree itself, throwing yourself sideways into the gorse bushes remembering to let go of the rope on landing. The toggle ropes had many uses; when joined together they could be fashioned into rope bridges, assist in scaling cliff faces. or overcoming other obstacles.

The next and possibly the most daunting obstacle was crossing over a single rope strung between two trees, one on each side of the river at a height of about fifteen feet. The idea was to pull yourself across by lying on the rope; this could be accomplished by hooking one foot behind you over the rope and allowing the free leg to act as a pendulum whilst pulling yourself along on your stomach. It was certainly more successful than trying to cross suspended below the rope by the arms. I know from experience having plummeted into a cold river a couple of times. The next crossing was a tree trunk laid from bank to bank, if you were to reach it before it got too wet your chances of crossing in one go were fairly good, however once it was wet and slippery you had to be very lucky to make it in one go.

Before getting to these obstacles, we had to negotiate some barbed wire by crawling through on our stomachs, all the while our friendly instructors were speeding us along with a few well placed thunder-flashes. Then we had to negotiate a cliff face about thirty feet high. All this had to be done at speed, so by the time it came to the rope crossings. we were feeling a little off balance. When tackling barbed wire as a group, it was easier for one member to throw himself across the triple rolls using his arms folded to protect his face avoiding the metal posts, and then allow the remainder of the group to use him as a bridge. It sounds a little suicidal but rarely did the bridge suffer any hurt. I know, because I was 'volunteered' on a number of occasion. It was not a matter of where there is no sense there is little feeling. As you lay on the wire and you felt the patter of ammunition boots running over your spine, the wire gave a little with each person crossing so by the time a dozen or more had used the facility, you could just pick yourself up off the wire, which by this time was flattened, and run to join your colleagues for the rest of the day's entertainment.

Two parallel ropes slung across the stream looked fairly easy. By tucking them under each arm and with your feet hooked over the ropes behind you, it was easy to make progress; that is with the proviso that you did not get too ambitious and reach just that little too far in front of you to have the rope suddenly slip from under one arm causing you to slip through the gap. With heavy ammunition pouches and webbing on, it was almost impossible to regain your position, leading almost inevitably to a descent into icy waters and starting all over again.

A footbridge crossed the stream further along, though we were not allowed to cross over it for fear of snipers, or so we were told.

Beneath the bridge was a metal strengthening rail about an inch in diameter. This was what we had to use to swing underneath. By gripping the rail in each hand and allowing one hand at a time to slide along as the body adopted a pendulum motion, it was possible to cross successfully from one side to the other. This, however, had to be learned the hard way and after a couple of unsuccessful attempts I finally realised that trying to use the Tarzan style did not work.

The last and final obstacle on that run before doing the whole lot in reverse was to allow yourself to drop from a humpback bridge into shallow water – not quite as easy as it sounds if you have to protect your legs and feet. I think that in the first few weeks that I was at *Armadillo*, I must have lost a stone and a half.

It would make a wonderful health farm in this day and age. However, I soon began to build up a few muscles after regularly going over the same course and getting a little faster each time. On a number of occasions we took part in night landings with some army detachments acting as the beach party responsible for handling the craft on the beach. This required the craft to be cleared into deeper water and away from the landing area, if 'hit' or in the event of an 'engine defect', two anomalies that our instructors arranged when they felt we were having an easy time.

To facilitate the removal of the damaged or defective craft, it was necessary to wade into the loch and bodily push the craft into deep water so that they could be towed away. Believe me when I tell you that the water in those lochs at that time of the year is chilly to say the least. One could hear the gasps as the water reached certain parts of the body. We began to wonder, could there be any truth in this brass monkey theory?

The other delightful exercise was a deepwater reconnaissance of the beach approaches in order to eliminate any possible underwater obstructions in the way of the landing craft, or deep holes where the poor bloody infantry man could stumble into after leaving the landing craft ramp with all his pack weighing him down. In this exercise we would join hands with tallest on the seaward end of the line, he would then wade into the water until he could keep his head just clear. Then we would turn and walk the whole length of the landing area, whilst the Beach Master made notes of the rise and fall of the reconnaissance party's progress. In this way he could produce a fairly reasonable chart of the area.

We were further instructed in the use of explosives that would enable us to remove obstructions, and bangalore-torpedos for blowing gaps in barbed wire entanglements. Cortex instantaneous fuse was used to cut though fallen trees and other barriers that might prevent exiting from the beach area to the hinterland. It was our job to see that a way was quickly cleared for the invading force to move over the beach area as quickly as possible.

Should any hold-ups occur, we were to communicate with the headquarters Command Ship lying off the beach so that they could regulate the landing craft, still having the option of using another beach. Therefore the use of beach signals was important to all of us. Each beach had its own designated morse signalling lamp and visual display of code. For instance the beach that I manned in Normandy was 'ITEM GREEN', the morse signalling lamp would be set to flash 'I' (--) This for the incoming landing craft to spot during the hours of darkness.

As an Assistant Beachmaster, my job entailed going in with the first assault wave with a bodyguard to cover me whilst I did a quick check of the beach to ascertain that we had arrived in the correct area. It was then necessary for me to get the information back to the headquarters ship to confirm the position. It could then be decided whether the landings would continue in that area. The first three waves would, out of necessity, be committed whatever happened, so one would always hope that we had got it right the first time. If not we would have to make our way to the designated area by whatever means was at our disposal.

On one of our night landing exercises, the instructing officer told me to take over from the coxswain of a Mark IV LCM. These were American built craft with a central wheel-house built over the engine room. The ramp had a solid section to the hull line and it looked like a bedstead with a frame work top to enable better vision. The noise in the wheelhouse was deafening with both engines going. There were separate hand controls to each engine, controlled direct from the wheel-house and, as I was approaching the beach, I found great difficulty in keeping over to starboard and had to correct my course a couple of times.

Eventually I beached the craft and successfully lowered the ramp in the right position. At that point the stoker came up on deck to report the port engine had stopped. The instruction officer, who happened to be the boat officer at *Armadillo*, asked the stoker how long had the engine been stopped. 'Soon after we got under way, Sir,' he replied. The instructor then turned to me and said, 'What was your job before being sent up here?' 'A Petty Officer Coxswain,' I replied. 'Well get out of there and let someone else have a go. You make it look too easy.'

The training necessary was rigorous; we were tested many times over the ten weeks that we were at Ardentinny. By the time that I had completed the course – which included unarmed combat, dealing with booby traps and, in general, staying alive – I felt that I could tackle anything. The whole course instilled a feeling of self confidence that I sometimes wish I possessed today.

Our very last exercise was a landing from an LCM at Loch Goilhead where we bivouacked overnight using a gas cape, a ground sheet and blanket. By pairing off we could make a reasonable tent by lacing the groundsheets together, and use the gas capes as insulation from the damp ground.

We washed and shaved using water direct from the loch and after a breakfast cooked over a small open fire, set in a small trench so that our mess tins rested on the edges and formed a tunnel thus giving a good draught to cook the better, we set out to return to Ardentinny. The first eight miles were on a good road and we made good time as we swung along with a few marching songs that helped to keep the pace going. However the next eight to ten miles seemed more like twenty, as we had to cross three hill ranges.

We set off in pairs so that we had someone who could, should an accident occur, assist you or get some help. It was tough going by any standard; there were sheer drops in places together with many boggy areas that could trap the unwary. We were not supplied with a map, and had not traversed this section before, so it was a matter of relying on our own sense of direction, and choosing the most direct route trying to avoid the worst of the terrain.

Our goal was reached in about six hours from the time that we had left Loch Goilhead. Wet through with sweat and aching in all our joints, we sought a nice hot bath in which to relax before enjoying a welcome and relaxing cup of tea back in the wardroom.

The six of us who had been sent to Ardentiny from Loch Ailort had all made it through the course with flying colours, and by way of celebration accepted an invitation from one of the wrens, who lived locally, to a dance in the village hall. I can honestly say that I did not know what I had let myself in for. We were 'heeling and toeing' for the best part of three hours, never being allowed to 'sit this one out' for the whole evening – the accordion, piano, and drums kept us on our feet, and the wrens took no prisoners.

If I hadn't known any different, I would have thought that the dance had been arranged as our last endurance test. The next day the calves of my legs felt like bars of iron, I could hardly walk without wincing. I certainly had a new respect for people who danced the Highland Fling from that day on.

# CHAPTER SIX
# 'J' COMMANDO

The day came when we received our postings to our Beach Parties, known as Commandos. Bob Campbell, a young Midshipman who had been one of the six that made up our course, was posted with me to 'J' Commando, which was then stationed in a little village outside Plymouth on the River Tamar, Tamerton Foliot.

Bob hailed from Halifax in Yorkshire and we were to become lasting friends, sharing quite a few adventures together. We travelled down by train from Glasgow, which seemed to take forever. It was a nightmare of a journey that took all of twenty-four hours, I think we must have gone round in circles during the night; I cannot even remember if we managed to get any food or refreshment whilst on that train. We were more than pleased to be met at the station by a wren driver with a utilicon to convey us to our new quarters.

On arrival at our new base, HMS *Foliot III*, we met our new colleagues; the officers and men of 'J' Commando. I was to be assistant beachmaster with 'J2' party, whilst Bob joined 'J3' in a similar capacity. The senior officer or beachmaster of 'J2' was Lt RNVR, 'Mac' McAuley, a Canadian of Scottish abstraction who was a bit of a romancer, though very easy to get along with. The other assistant beachmaster was a young midshipman RNVR, Ray Summers, who hailed from Kent. The other officers of 'J' were Lt RNVR Bill Lindsey, the beachmaster of 'J1', with midshipman RNVR Pete Snelling, and midshipman RNVR Phil Lord as his assistant beachmasters. The beachmaster of 'J3' was Lt RNVR Ronnie Wheeler, a local man from Newton Abbot, who, prior to the war, was with Customs and Excise. His other assistant beachmaster was Sub-Lt RNVR Bill Stephens, who hailed from Plymouth.

Each party consisted of twenty seamen, including two leading seamen, two petty officers, a lieutenant as commanding officer, and two junior officers assisting. The Commando comprised of three such parties, making a total of sixty-six other ranks and eleven officers, 'J' was still short of a principal beachmaster, usually a lieutenant commander, and an assistant principal beachmaster usually filled by a sub-lieutenant. As these posts had not been filled to date, Lt Bill Lindsay was the acting PBM.

I soon fell into the routine training that kept the Commando on its toes. We had a twice-weekly run over the assault course set up along the bank of the nearby River Tamar. This was every bit as demanding as that at Ardentinny. On two days of the week, we had a twelve-mile cross country run that had to be completed in two hours if you wanted to be back at camp in time to catch the first 'liberty boat'.

Wednesdays were always allocated to an all-day route march with full pack and equipment; this always consisted of twenty minutes marching, twenty minutes double time, and twenty minutes marching again with a five minute break on the hour. We must have covered the whole of Devon and nearby Cornwall during our spell at Tamerton Foliot. Interspaced with these activities were little stunts, like a march to Dawlish and back in two days. The local landing craft unit was used to put us ashore at Whitsand Bay, leaving us to march forty miles to St Dominick, near Bere Alston, where we could ford the River Tamar and then make our way back to Tamerton Foliot, which was another ten miles or so.

This was in December, so we had to keep moving to keep warm. I should add that we started at dusk, and we did stop at a local for an hour before closing time. The senior medical officer at Tamerton decided that he would like to come with us to see what we had to put up with. He opted out when we left the pub. By then, we were in such a position that we could not opt for a shortcut over the Tamar Bridge.

When we did have our breaks of five minutes, it was always agony to get started again on our blistered feet. On taking my boots off when we arrived back in camp, some twenty-four hours after we had left, it was to find that I had blisters that reached from toe to heel on both feet. I went to the bathroom and lay in a nice hot bath utterly exhausted, only to be awakened some time later, when the bath was cold, by one of the other resident officers at the camp who had heard me snoring. He had physically shaken me after climbing over a partition wall.

We also carried out normal naval routines, such as being duty officer when our turn of duty came round or guard commander for morning division and colours. Soon after joining 'J', PBM Lt-Com. Bell RNVR joined, together with his assistant, Sub-Lt Tom Hewitt RNVR, who hailed from Rotherhithe, and who, like myself, was an ex-landing barge petty officer coxswain. Obviously we got on very well together. We had a lot of mutual friends though had not previously met one another.

Tom was probably around the thirty mark, age-wise, and was married with a couple of children. He had been awarded the British Empire Medal for rescue work in the Surrey Commercial Docks during the Blitz on that first daylight raid on Saturday 7 September 1941, when millions of tons of timber were destroyed. He was tough but gentlemanly in character. His father had been a one-time judo and wrestling champion in his younger days; Tom had obviously picked up some of his skills. We worked together to train the lads in unarmed combat. My part in the team was that of the 'fall-guy'; rarely, did I get the opportunity to reverse that role. Tom was very quick to counter any move of mine. I soon found that it was better to learn how to fall when thrown, and how to roll back onto my feet.

The senior petty officer in 'J2' was William Fedder, an advanced gunnery instructor who had spent a great deal of his service at Whale Island, the home of foot drill and gunnery in the Royal Navy. He was a tough, experienced man who was invaluable in the running and training of the party. Like his counterpart, Petty Officer Tunnely, he was a regular General Service rating. These two men held the respect of both officers and men alike. It followed that a lot of thought had gone into their selection for Commando service.

Whilst out for my first cross country run with the commando, in the usual PT vest and shorts, I found myself running alongside a lad whom I recognised as my old corporal from when I was in the Home

Guard back at South Benfleet in 1941. He seemed a little surprised to see me and asked how long I had been with 'J', then said that he would look me up later in the day, when we returned to camp. I discovered that he was a leading seaman with 'J1' party. He was taken aback when he discovered I was the duty officer inspecting the liberty men that afternoon.

We spent Christmas at Tamerton Foliot that year; I had sought, and got, permission to take Bob Campbell with me for a long weekend leave to my home. We were to travel on Christmas Day – apparently this was to allow the civilian population to have the transport on Christmas Eve; there was over crowding when too many service personnel were on the move. All had been arranged but I turned my ankle whilst doing a Tuesday run over the assault course and then developed a sore throat and headache that evening. Wednesday was the normal all day route march and 'Mac' Macaully, my CO, decided that I had better miss that out and stay behind.

I was still in my bunk at 0830 when I was roused by the duty officer, who informed me that the commander wanted to see me in his office, and to get there as soon as possible. As quickly as I could I made my way to the commanders' office. After knocking at the door, I was bade to enter. I removed my cap and was quickly told to keep it on. I stood to attention in front of his desk wondering what I had done. 'What were you doing still in your bunk at 0800?' he demanded. I replied that I had been excused the route march because of a turned ankle and that I had been unwell with a sore throat and headache. He made a quick phone call, then told me to report to the sick bay.

I was met by the senior medical officer who asked, 'What have you been up to?' 'I don't know' I replied, and explained to him what had happened. He confirmed my ankle was sprained and that I had septic tonsils. Writing out a note and handing it to me, he said, 'Give this to the commander'. I reported back to the commander's office and handed him the note. He looked at it and then said, 'That is no excuse for you still being in your bunk at 0800. You will be required for duty on board for the next seven days.' I was dumbstruck. That was our Christmas leave wiped off in one stroke.

I went back to the room that the Commando officers shared, a large Nissen hut. On approaching my bunk, the lower of two (Bob Campbell occupied the top berth), I spotted a note left for the steward, informing him that I was not to be wakened. It read 'DO NOT SHAKE', in large letters. I had not noticed this before, and wondered who on earth had put it there.

I eventually found the answer when the Commando returned from the route march. Bob Campbell came bouncing in, all smiles, and said, 'Did you have a good sleep Jack? I left a note on your bunk so that you would not be disturbed.' It was then that I told him what had happened and the consequences about my leave being stopped. In a typical Yorkshire way, he said, 'Ee! He can't do that, I am going to tell him what happened.' Taking the note, he made for the door. I did try to warn him not to go, but it was too late; he had already gone.

A little time elapsed, and then Bob came back into the hut, his face as long as a fiddle. We did not have to ask how had he got on. By this time, everyone in the hut knew of the story. 'What happened, Bob?' was the chorus, 'I am required to stay on board for seven days' he replied. 'What did he say about the note?' 'If Gaster cannot get up under his own steam, then he deserves to stay on board,' he replied, 'and I am not to leave any more notes in future.' Well, that was our long weekend up the creek. Christmas and Boxing Day would be spent on board.

Christmas day arrived and we were all required to attend a service in the nearby church where we sang carols with the congregation before returning to the canteen, where drinks were on the mess before going to have our traditional Christmas dinner. I can remember Bob and I propping up the corner of the bar 'drowning our sorrows', before going in to the mess to eat our dinner. After that, it was a bit of a blank. It seemed almost like a dream sequence, with me being made to stand in the canteen and then subsiding back into a chair.

When I eventually arrived back in the land of the living, it was to find myself lying in my bunk in a somewhat dazed condition. I must have uttered a groan, which was answered by another from the bunk above. It was dark and we were alone in the hut, 'What has happened?' I asked Bob, who was occupying his bunk. 'We are under close arrest for conduct unbecoming officers and gentlemen,' he replied, I was stunned. I gathered myself together and went into the washroom to freshen up, and then looked at my uniform jacket and could see a tear in it where the top button had been pulled away but had been repaired in a fairly neat way. 'What happened to my jacket?' I asked. 'Who sewed it up for me?' 'It was torn when you were made to stand up in the canteen,' he replied. 'You did the repair work yourself.'

The following morning, Bob and I were brought before the commander; I was the first one to be dealt with. I was told that I had acted in a way unbecoming an officer and that, If I could not hold my drink, then I could do without it for the next month, when I would be required for duty on board. My wine bill would be stopped with immediate effect. I apologised for my behaviour and accepted the punishment, then returned to my quarters, Bob followed a little later a little indignant that he had collected the same punishment thinking that he had not been drunk at all. That is, until Ron Wheeler his CO in 'J3', said, 'Well, if you will go chasing the wrens across the parade ground flapping your arms like a bird, and shouting goosey goosey! What can you expect?' Things were not so bad. Whenever I had a 'soft' drink in the canteen, somehow or other it always had that special something in it. Though I never had more than one, and I always made it last.

I was duty officer on the gate on New Year's Eve and supervised the ringing out of 1943, and the ringing in of 1944. It was eight bells for each, sixteen in all, and as per custom, it was done by the youngest rating on board. There was I, feeling old at twenty! At about 0130, the commander appeared, driving home in his car. He lived in the village. Winding down his window as I saluted him, he called out, 'Goodnight and a happy new year,' as he drove somewhat over carefully through the gates.

We had a number of exercises that entailed the Commando being dropped twenty-odd miles by covered lorries. We were told that we were the 'enemy', and that the home guard and local police had been informed of our presence, and were out to prevent us getting back to the camp.

Fortunately for us, most of the area we knew like the backs of our hands. We had covered it during our route marches, though we did have one funny incident when seeking cover whilst bypassing a village. We took to a dry ditch alongside a hedgerow, and several of our group proceeded to crawl along it, making as little noise as possible, when a rustling noise was heard on the other side of the hedge. It was dusk and the light was fading. As I was in the lead, I signalled for silence, then peeked through the leaves to find two big eyes and a white face looking at me. I very nearly fell over. It was the face of a cow that was seeking the shelter of the hedge. She was as surprised to see me, as I was by her. She trotted away, thankfully not making any noise. I think that the Home Guard had packed up and gone home for their tea.

On another exercise we carried out on Dartmoor, our opponents then were 'E' Commando. I was advancing with a group from 'J2' to a point where we had to cross a railway line. I was, I thought, very careful to keep a low profile as we moved across the track when an umpire waved to us and said, 'You lot are all casualties.' 'How come?' I asked. 'They' he said pointing to a hedgerow some fifty yards away, 'have been targeting you with mortars for a couple of minutes.' 'What happens now?' 'Go down to the Hotel over there. You will find the rest of the casualties.' When we arrived, it was to see a good few of both Commandos happily supping a few jars at the bar. The rest of the afternoon was spent meeting old and new friends. In the end, I quite liked that umpire; I think that he knew what was good for me.

Not long after this, we were on the move again, but not before the commander called Bob and me in to see him and wish us well. He wasn't such a bad old stick. First, we returned to Armadillo, our home base, from where we were allowed to take some leave after a reassessment of our proficiency together. A few replacements also came to Armadillo, because some of the lads had been promoted to leading seamen etc. Whilst we were there, Mac McAuley went on leave and failed to rejoin us. I never discovered what happened, though I did hear that he went to Ireland and for some reason was brought back under escort after we had left for our new base at South Queensferry, HMS *Hopetoun*.

# CHAPTER SEVEN

# SOUTH QUEENSFERRY

HMS *Hopetoun*, our new base, was very close to a naval patrol service base, Port Edgar. The men were all housed in Nissen huts; the officers' wardroom was shared with the staff of the base in a nice building that I can imagine had been a large country manor. It was very comfortable, and what is more, we were able to visit Edinburgh whilst on shore leave. Also, there was a nice little pub almost under the Forth Bridge, The Hawes Inn, well within walking distance for a nice quiet evening ashore. I was beginning to feel quite at home in Scotland.

The routine training carried on. Petty Officer Fedder and myself set about rigging up an assault course to keep the lads on their toes. A nearby valley with a cliff face at one end provided a most suitable site to rig our death slide. We had a suitable tree near the top of the cliff and one at the bottom, though it was a little further than we would have liked. The rope supplied was in 120-fathom coils – standard issue from the stores. We secured the rope around the tree at the top with a clove hitch two half hitches and a lashing to ensure it would not slip. But there was insufficient length of rope left to secure it to the lower tree. We thought of splicing on another shorter length, though this would have entailed using a long splice and may have restricted the toggle ropes sliding down smoothly.

A word with the storekeeper and we were soon in possession of a 3-inch 150-fathom flexible steel wire rope. We were in business.

Once rigged in position, I decided that I should do the test run before committing any of the lads to it. It was a far longer slide than any that we had undertaken before, and by the time we neared the bottom, the wire rope dipped enough to make a running landing on the grassy patch about fifteen feet from the end. It was 'hairy' but safe enough. After a couple of runs, we noticed that the toggle ropes were beginning to chafe through.

Petty Officer Fedder came up with the idea of getting a shackle big enough to use directly on the wire, with the toggle rope through this. The idea was ok, and as he had come up with it, he decided that he should be the test pilot on this occasion. It certainly got over the chafing of the ropes, but his speed on the descent was almost doubled. When he hit the ground running he was moving too fast to stop and made a pretty poor landing, bouncing along a few yards. He was stunned for a while, and had managed to put a fountain pen that he carried in his battledress pocket through the flesh of his cheek. He tried to make light of it, but I insisted that he go to the sick bay for a check-up, he was detained overnight for observation which upset him as he had a date with one of the wren drivers that evening. I promised that I would see that she was informed and I believe he had an unexpected visit from her, which he was very happy about.

The wire slide was dismantled; we did not want too many casualties. We tried to think of other ways to keep ourselves amused without breaking our necks. One of the tried and tested keep-fit exercises was a game called 'Brighton Football.' This was played using a medicine ball. The two sides were picked from the twenty men in 'J2' with Petty Officer Fedder on one side, myself on the other, and Petty Oofficer Tunnely as referee, the rules, if rules existed, were to get the ball through the opposition's goal in any way you chose. To mark the two sides, the ones in vests were my team, and those not in vest were the opposition. It always amazed me that whenever I or P.O. Fedder managed to get the ball, we always finished up at the bottom of a huge scrum. I wonder if we had upset them. Were getting a little of their own back?

Several times we went out for night exercises, mostly to live rough on our twenty-four hour ration packs to see how we could manage. By this time Lt Bill Stevens had taken over as CO of 'J2'. He was a very easy man to get on with, and was instantly liked by the lads. It transpired that he had taken part in the landings at Anzio, where the beaches had come under some intense fire and bombing. He showed the lads how to live off the land and with some foraging we manage a fair old stew using a couple of tins of bully beef.

At about this time, we went to the little seaport of Musselburgh, where I was delighted to meet some of my old landing barge flotilla, Jimmy Jewiss and Stan Everard in particular. I asked them how they had found their way up to Scotland, and it seemed they had been transported by an LSD, a Landing Ship Dock, very similar to the present-day assault ships used by the Royal Marine Commandos. Very soon after this, we took part in an exercise at Gullane Beach near North Berwick. This is where we encountered the DUKWs for the first time.

What marvelous vehicles they were. This was to be proved during the storms of 'D'+19 in Normandy, when a number of the LBVs were swamped. They were the only craft moving in and out of the beaches collecting vital ammunition and stores from the ships within and outside the Mulberry Harbour, but I will deal with more of that later.

We were impressed with their versatility – eight knots on water, sixty mph plus on shore, three tons load on water, and I believe ten on land. The tyre's could be inflated or deflated according to the nature of the surface on which the vehicle was travelling. The propeller and pump were operated with a separate set of gear levers. I was envious; all we had was an amphibious Jeep that could only manage four knots on water so long as it wasn't choppy, and if that was case, the air intake vent had to be closed and the engine overheated. Though to be fair it did have a dinky little winch on the bonnet, and it held the road well on dry land.

We were well equipped with some Lanchesters. These were modified sten guns with furniture and bayonet fittings, and were used by the bodyguards, whose job it was to look after the ABMs whilst they were busy carrying out reconnaissance. A stripped Lewis was for ack-ack use or to be fired from the hip when necessary. Short Lee Enfield rifles 303, were used by half the party, whilst those whose job it was to tote the signalling equipment had Smith and Wesson 4.55 revolvers, this included the officers. They were heavy old First World War weapons, with a six-inch barrel, they were fairly accurate at thirty yards, and packed a punch if they struck home.

We had plenty of instruction in the use of hand grenades, including the safe priming of these weapons. All too many accidents have occurred by holding the detonators in a warm hand or crimping them by using the teeth. Our lads were too valuable to the Commando to be lost through carelessness. Another weapon at hand was the bakelite bomb, used mainly for stun purposes, though again, if used carelessly, it could cause severe injury. We were also trained in the use of the beehive bomb, so named, I believe, because of its shape. When placed on the outside wall of a pillbox or gun emplacement, it could blast a hole in the wall of sufficient size that would allow a grenade to be introduced if the initial blast had failed to incapacitate the occupiers.

By the beginning of February 1944, we were in a state of readiness for anything we were asked to do. The whole Commando was then granted a seven-day home leave. I think this was to relax us a wee bit before the coming task. On our return to Scotland, a number of briefings were given to the officers regarding target areas that had been selected with up to date information supplied by the Combined Operations Pilotage Personnel, and from our friends in the French Resistance.

Such information would be, for example, photographs taken of the shoreline from submarines operating offshore, samples of sand or gravel collected from the beaches by the use of a rubber dinghy, and information regarding underwater obstacles, defensive works and mined areas. Lives had been risked in obtaining this information that was of immense value to the people whose job it was to secure the beachhead.

Life went on much the same for a while – intensive training and exercise with the occasional visit into Edinburgh for an evening out. I was mostly content to venture only as far as the Hawes Inn for a couple of pints and then stroll back to our quarters on the right side of midnight for a good night's rest. Plans were made for a dance to be held in the nearby base with 'J' commando as hosts. Tickets were printed for sometime in June. It was something that everyone was eager to attend and no doubt word was spread far and wide.

As we approached the end of April, I was called in to see the PBM, who said 'I know that you will be disappointed, but I want you to take charge of the second wave of the Commando to land. As you are the

Jack Gaster with Commando unit, (seated, second from left).

senior sub-lieutenant, I will leave you with two midshipmen and twenty hands. You will be our back up and fill in any gaps left by casualties.' I was a bit gutted, to say the least, but I suppose it was a responsibility that had to be filled by someone. I had Phil Lord and Bob Campbell as my assistants, so in a way I was classed as a deputy beachmaster.

In May we all took part in photographic session. The three parties, 'J1', 'J2' and 'J3', were photographed seperately and then the whole Commando was gathered together. Then, with little warning, we were entrained south to a sealed camp on the outskirts of Southampton, where, once inside, we were not allowed out without an escort. The whole camp was surrounded by barbed wire and guarded by armed sentries who had orders to shoot anyone attempting to break out. We had all been briefed as to our roles, so there was a need for rigid security, so much so that I had to accompany a petty officer from 'J1' party to a dentist while he had treatment for trench mouth and stay in the treatment room with him to ensure that he did not divulge any information that could have been of any use to the enemy.

We spent nearly four weeks in the camp shared by many army units, including some Canadian lads from Princess Pat's Highland

Light Infantry. They all appeared to be six-footers, full of life and eager to go. I came across a group of them one day preparing their grenades for use. They were using their teeth to crimp the detonators, so I hurried on, not wishing to spoil their fun or deal with any casualties that might occur. Towards the end of May, sections of the Commando left the camp. They were there one minute, then away the next. There were no goodbyes, just vacant tents, and a sense of uncertainty.

At the beginning of June, my turn came. By this time, the original plan to leave me with the party of twenty plus the midshipmen had been cancelled. We were now split up between the three parties again, but put aboard different landing craft so that at least a proportion of the beach parties would survive the initial landings to take over control of the landing areas. I was to find myself with the APBM and about a dozen men from 'J2' on an LST. The large queues of vehicles making for the hard at Hythe seemed to take forever, we were marshalled onto craft that seemed hungry, eager to fill their vast interiors with as much of the trucks, bren-gun carriers, and halftracks as they could cope with.

Once laden, we moved out into the Solent, where we found ourselves surrounded by a vast armada of grey ships and landing craft. Once there, we lay at anchor for what seemed a long time, though it may only have been twenty-four hours or so. I got my head down when I was not required to do rounds of the troop's accommodation, which lined the ship's flanks below decks. Everyone seemed in good spirits. Maybe there was a little false bravado here and there. Then we felt the ship begin to move, and we were on our way.

Some of the men we were sharing this trip with had seen it all before. I, on the other hand, was going to my baptism of fire. How was I going to react? I said a little silent prayer: 'Dear God, if I do collect one, make it quick and clean, I would like to reach my twenty-first birthday in August, and Lord, I haven't "dipped my wick" yet.' Silly thing to say, but I guess it mattered.

# CHAPTER EIGHT

# NORMANDY

An amazing sight met our eyes when we eventually came on deck on the morning of 6 June. The initial landings had already gone in and we could hear the bombardment long before we arrived in the holding area. I watched as the heavy guns of the monitor HMS *Roberts* fired its shells, weighing a ton apiece, over the landing area. It was possible to watch their flight over the beaches. As we approached the landing site, we could see the wreckage of damaged landing craft where they had hit beach obstructions that had mines attached to them. It then struck me that we were coming in on the wrong beach as far as 'J' Commando was concerned. This was 'KING' beach in the Courselles area, already manned by 'R' Commando. As soon as we cleared the LST, I arranged with the beachmaster for a lift with an LCM Mk 1 – the British version – to 'ITEM GREEN' Beach at Le Hamel.

I was upset to see quite a few young Canadian bodies in the shallow waters off 'KING' beach. They had never made it ashore to use those grenades that they were tossing to one another like toys just a few days before.

As we approached Le Hamel, we could see some of the block ships being sunk in position to protect the beachhead. This was the beginnings of the Mulberry Harbour. Our coxswain lay offshore a bit as we passed the sanatorium by Le Hamel. There was still quite a bit of activity and firing in that corner, but we dodged between obstacles, and were eventually brought onto the beach near the western end, where a chalk cliff separated us from Arromanches.

We quickly scrambled ashore where we were met by our colleagues from 'J' who had landed with the assault wave. They had already established a sheltered position for the Beachmasters HQ. It was sited on a sand ridge running along the top of the beach, beyond which lay a flooded area surrounded by barbed wire, with signs proclaiming 'Achtung Minen'. Looking along the base of the wire, we could see strands of fine wire disappearing into the sand along its length. These were attached to Teller mines. As we did not wish to cross the wire at that point we left them very much alone.

Members of the Landing Craft Obstacle Clearing Units (LCOCU) were busy doing their dangerous work, making the beaches safe for the landing craft, who were coming in an endless stream to disgorge military hardware onto the beaches. In the meantime, the Royal Engineers' beach recovery tanks and bulldozers were clearing the hedgehog obstacles away from the beaching areas.

Other tanks fitted with flails were busy clearing a path through the field that lay to the right of the beach and continued uphill to a point

Beachmasters HQ 1944.

where it joined a road through to Arromanches. These were closely followed by another tank with a roll of Sommerfeld Tracking that unrolled as it made its way uphill, making a steel mesh roadway as it progressed. Meanwhile, as the sounds of battle receded away from the beach area, we took stock of our position. A bivouac area close to a dry-stone wall that had been checked for mines by members of the Royal Engineers was chosen for a tented site. Senior Petty Officer Bill Fedder soon had this organised for us with half a dozen ridge tents to house 'J1' and 'J2' parties. 'J3' were on the other side of the chalk cliff, in Arromanches itself.

Watches were arranged to cover the duties on the beach itself, in a four on, four off routine. Bob Campbell and I shared watches. The midday and afternoon, watches were always busy, though we were governed by the tides once the LBVs and PBRs started to come in. The PBRs were the army version of the LBVs. They were called Power Barge Ramps. These craft were offloading the ships that were now beginning to arrive off the beachhead. Each ship carried up to fifty tons or more in its hold and required the high tide to swing, so that their ramp was facing inshore. It would then settle on the beach as the ebb set in. The ships were then unloaded with lorries that were using the metal road created by the engineers.

While they occupied the eastern side of the beach, we had the DUKWs coming and going throughout the whole tide cycle. I am beginning to realise now that because of my experience as an LBV coxswain and my river work on the Thames, I was in the best position to assist my old colleagues. Come to think of it, it was like a giant game of draughts. I am glad that I was on the winning side.

One very sad incident occured while I was on duty one afternoon. An RAF corporal approached me to ask where he and two airmen could bivouac in safety; they had been taking charge of balloons brought over by the landing craft which would be used to set up a defence against enemy aircraft in the Mulberry Harbour area. I advised them to see the Royal Engineer Captain in charge of the beach area, as he would know of the cleared areas. Shortly afterward, I spotted them along the other side of the beach exit. They seemed to be coping well. I turned to look at a DUKW that was coming toward me from the roadway, and I sensed rather than heard an explosion. Turning my head in their direction, I saw, almost in slow motion, their bodies lifted and thrown in a ghastly pirouette. Two were killed outright, the other survived for an hour. I was shaken by this incident, and the question always remained with me: could I have done more for these lads?

In the meantime, the Mulberry Harbour was beginning to take shape. The concrete sections were being delivered and sunk into place, forming a sheltered area from Le Hamel in the east to the west side of Arromanches, closing the gaps left by the sunken ships (gooseberries) that formed the original breakwater early on D-Day. Sections of the Phoenix Piers were being moved into place and held in position by the dropping of the 'spuds', the suspended steel piles at each corner of the floating sections that held the piers in position at all states of tide. Then the floating roadway sections were manoeuvered into position by the TID tugs of the IWT section of the Royal Engineers, to form the link between the piers and the shore.

Petty Officer Fedder did sterling work supplying small explosive charges with which he was able to blast holes in the beach large enough to push clump and mushroom anchors of sufficient size, securing the piers to the shore in the shortest possible time. Once this was done, vessels could offload their cargos directly onto the lorries on the pier itself, and then the cargo would be driven directly to its destination, the forward supply depots.

Another pier was positioned on the western section of our beach, from which mostly military vehicles were offloaded from LSTs. They were driven away from the beach area using the Sommerfeld Tracking laid across the field to the rear of the beach area. Once, when I was making for our bivouac area, having been relieved from my watch as beachmaster, I was walking along the original gravel road when a DUKW was making its way down to the beach. I stepped up onto the grass verge that was a little higher than the road surface to give him more room to pass a bren-gun carrier that had already left the beach and was following some ten yards behind me. The carrier moved over to my side of the road and put his track onto the verge to allow the DUKW to pass. In that instant, there was an explosion that blew his track right off. I was lucky not to have been hit by flying metal when that happened. I had to ask myself: what if I had triggered that blast when I walked along that same spot?

A few days after this incident, a flail tank started to clear the field that lay on the other side of the dry-stone wall behind our tented bivouac area. Immediately, several 'S' mines were detonated. These were rather nasty anti-personnel devices, triggered by someone kicking against one of the three small prongs situated on the top of the mine. It would be fired from a metal cup that was buried in the soil, causing it to be lifted about four feet from the ground before exploding with a killing range of about fifty feet. Our immediate concern was the damage done to our tents; those alongside the wall were damaged by the flying shrapnel contained within the body of the mine.

Petty Officer Fedder brought several of these into the bivouac area and proceeded to take them apart. Needless to say, there was a general exodus from the vicinity he was working in. I suppose I should have had my head examined; I was so fascinated that I stayed to watch as he unscrewed the detonator. It would take a very sharp eye to spot the three little prongs in a grass-covered area. He lifted the mine proper from its metal case, which was some five inches in diameter and six inches in depth. This was the part that remained in the ground and acted as mortar. He then dismantled the mine casing and poured out the contents. There were over 200 pieces of rod iron that had been cut at forty-five degrees, measuring about half an inch long from one sharp end to the other. There was no wonder that they were so deadly.

The flail tank carried on its task of clearing the field, gradually moving further away, but the damage had been done to two tents, including that shared by myself and Bill Stephens. There had been a couple of sneak raids by 'Jerry', so I thought it prudent to make a small sheltered dugout on similar lines to the Anderson shelters that I had reason to be thankful for. I collected some sandbags and oddments of timber from the beach and set about making my new quarters near to the galley, an old wooden caravan and a tarpaulin tent that our two 'able seamen cooks' had fashioned around their cooking area. I was able to make use of some empty Compo ration boxes to line the interior of the dugout, these made good cupboards.

I will admit that I was extra vigilant when digging the earth away from the inside of the shelter, and used my fingers to suss out any suspicious objects. I was pleased with my handiwork. The interior measured some eight feet in length when finished, and six feet in width. The roof consisted of two old wooden doors supported at each end by four logs and pieces of driftwood. I found some more short lengths of logs, which I split to line the end wall, giving it a log cabin effect. The entrance was affected by empty Compo ration boxes filled with soil and placed one on top of the other on either side, with sand bags on the outside. Finally, there was a blast wall of sandbags across the entrance. It must have been adequate, as Bill Stephens decided to become my lodger.

Most of the lads from 'J2' had fashioned themselves protective living quarters, some in the footings of a bungalow that had been demolished long before we arrived. Others got a friendly bulldozer driver to dig a fairly wide trench, then roofed it over with old sleepers, a tarpaulin, and sandbags. Tom Hewitt and Lt-Com. Bell had set up their headquarters in a pill box that dominated the other end of the beach, where there was a narrow exit to a road that went into Le Hamel. There was a large sanatorium nearby. Communications were a little primitive – field telephones sometimes had wires damaged by vehicles, the radio packs needed two men to operate. They took it in turn to carry the rather bulky sets on their backs.

Tom Hewitt called on me one day, soon after Bayeux had been liberated, to accompany him on a trip there. The beach was then being covered by my opposite number, so I readily agreed. We got a lift in with one of the large army trucks that regularly plied to and from the beach. It was pitiful to see the large numbers of dead animals with swollen carcasses in the fields as we made our way into the town. On arrival, we were greeted in a very friendly manner, though we were always on our guard in case any unfriendly elements were about. I purchased some cheese and was encouraged to have my photograph taken. I was told that it would be ready in the hour.

On returning to collect it, I vowed never to attempt growing a beard again. I had not shaved for three weeks, and my head had been shorn before I left the sealed camp in Southampton. I looked a sight. The razor came out as soon as I got back to my dugout. While we were on our way back to the beach, we passed a bulldozer who left the Sommerfeld Tracking for some reason, possibly to make room for the large truck on which we were travelling. Unfortunately, the driver was killed when his track triggered a mine. His cabin was penetrated by shrapnel.

Soon after returning to the beach, the weather began to deteriorate with strong to gale-force winds. The harbour had not been completed on the western side, where the wind was strongest, so heavy swells began to run through the gaps and onto the beach. A number of LBVs and PBRs that were beached were being smothered by the breaking seas that penetrated the gaps. Those that were underway within the harbour sought the shelter of the block ships and Phoenix units and moored secure against them.

As the tide rose that evening, the craft on the beach were swamped before they could kedge themselves off into deep water. The crews had to be taken off; they jumped into lorries that backed up close as possible to them. On one that lay a little further out, I got a DUKW to take me along. It was tricky; one moment we were lifted high, with the danger of being dashed against the barge, the next we were almost level.

The DUKWs only had very thin hulls, which would have torn open if in contact with the heavily built barges. Forty barges were swamped and sunk on the beaches during the four days that the gale raged, and we must be thankful that the DUKWs kept going the whole time, with the loss of only one, which tore its side out against an obstruction. They were worth their weight in gold for keeping the ammunition supply coming ashore from the ships. It was from one of these DUKW's that Bobby Campbell made what I think was a very brave attempt to divert a mine from being swept onto one of the ammunition ships outside the harbour.

On one of these ships, someone reported what they thought was a mine being swept by the tide onto their vessel. It was certainly a metal object lying deep in the water. Bob got one of the DUKW drivers to put him as close as possible, then he dived over the side to push it clear of the ship. It turned out to be a smoke float, but Bob did not know that before he got to it. If I had been the PBM, I would have recommended Bob for a medal or a mention in dispatches, but from what I heard, it was looked at as a joke.

A whole lot of damage was done to the craft around the beaches and I was called to go with a party of ten men from 'J2' to assist in getting some timbers placed under the keel of the destroyer HMS

*Fury,* which had been driven ashore against a cliff face near Port-en-Bessin. It reminded me of our salvage work in Poole Harbour. We dug away gravel in a number of places and slid huge bulks of timber, on which were placed rollers, to assist with her re-launching. There was a lot of fuel oil that had escaped from her bilges, and we were somewhat smothered in a sticky tarry mess by the time we had finished. I got our driver to divert to a large Army quartermasters store on the way back to our beach; there we managed to get some new battledress jackets and trousers to replace our soiled ones. The PBM was a little bit worried as to whose slop chit they would appear on. I signed for them and I have not had a bill to date.

Once the storm had subsided, plans were drawn up to ensure that craft for discharge on the beach should be provided with secure moorings, to prevent a repetition of the damage caused by their anchors failing to hold them. It was decided that we would lay three trots of buoys so that we could secure them head and astern, both on the spring and neap tides. I was delegated, with Tom Hewitt and petty officer Fedder and the assistance of one of the LBE's crews, to do the work. I should say that during the gale, a drifting LBV was washed up onto the beach while I was on duty one night. I was able, with the help of my lads, to refloat it and moor it inside one of the Phoenix units. Unfortunately its stars-and-stripes flag became dislodged while we were busy salvaging it, and the paint around its official number was chafed beyond recognition.

I had to claim salvage rights and repaint it with the RNBC 'J' on its transom. After all, a sailor without a ship is a sight indeed. We were in business to retrieve the salvaged cases of tinned food that were drifting around the harbour. We had been living on Compo rations for too long. So now we were able to bring in the necessary cable and mushroom anchors from a boom defence vessel lying outside the harbour. The splicing of the wire was done on board the LBE. We made three lengths of five-inch cable in lengths of 100 fathoms, each with two clump anchors at each end, set at forty-five degrees from the end, and clump anchors at twenty fathom intervals on either side. These were where the mooring buoys were attached so that the craft could lay moored fore and aft according to whether it was a spring or neap tide.

Trying to dig holes in which to bury the anchors was nigh impossible. The sea water would seep into the hole, bringing in the sand before the anchor could be placed. This is where Petty Officer Fedder came into his own. He produced ten-pound charges that he had made up from captured ammunition and all we had to do was dig a hole small enough for his charge, then walk a safe distance away while he had a bulldozer driver on hand to pull the anchors in position. In no time at all, we were in business. While this was going on, the Royal Engineers IWT captain, responsible for the LBVs on our beach, arranged to have a repair base close to the pillbox. Thus he needed to be out of the way, as he wanted vehicle access to that end of the beach. Agreement was reached, so preparations were made to demolish the pillbox using a 100 lb charge.

With a 100 lb charge timed to blow the debris out to sea, it was decided that a quarter-mile safety zone would be sufficient. The day came when this was going to happen and the beach was cleared of personnel. The countdown started, then came an explosion far in excess of that envisaged. A column of dust and debris spread around, some pieces falling half a mile away. Apparently, under the floor of the pillbox, which appeared to be clay, lay a vast magazine that had been set off by the blast. Maybe it was a good thing that both Tom and Lt-Com. Bell were non smokers.

A few days after completing the beach moorings for the barges, I noticed a Royal Engineers mine clearance team working in a section to the right of the beach exit road, just clear of the beach. It had been marked off with the normal white tapes denoting it as uncleared and with the usual 'Achtung Minen' sign on the wire around the area. Apparently, these were known as 'shoe' mines, and were undetectable using the ordinary detectors because they were constructed of wood and the detonator was brass, with just a small nail that activated the pull action of the detonator when it was pressed down. It was shaped like a small shoe box (hence the name), which was hinged at one end, with one lid raised about an inch above the other. Here, a narrow opening, about a half an inch across, was cut so that it fitted over the end of the fuse where the nail was passed through an eye in the pull section of the fuse. The end of the lid was shaped like a wedge and this, when forced down, acted as the trigger.

The only way that the R.E.s could locate them was by pushing long steel rods through the soil at an angle until they found something solid, and then very carefully scraping away the soil around them. They were highly sensitive, having been buried for quite a long time, apparently during the British evacuation, although this was not verified. Within a few minutes they claimed their first victim, a young sapper who was badly injured around the face and eyes, then the sergeant had to try to rally his now shaken unit. A Field Ambulance Unit removed the injured man, and the young subaltern who remained with the unit decided that he would have a go, again with disastrous results. By this time the IWT Captain responsible for the beach area called a halt, telling them to pack up, saying 'I don't know whose idea it was to clear that part. We are not using it, and I shall use a flail tank to clear it later.'

Just a few nights later, round about 11.00 p.m., Bill Stephens and I were relaxing in our shelter in just shirt and trousers ready for some 'shut eye' when I heard a low flying plane fairly close. 'One of ours' I said, 'No! That's a Jerry' said Bill, and hardly had the words left his mouth than we heard the 'Weeeee' of the falling bomb, and felt the thud of it hitting the ground. 'It's alright,' I ventured, 'it's a delay'; again I was mistaken.

There was an almighty bang, and we felt clods of earth striking the shelter, with some pieces finding the doorway. Then we could hear a series of smaller explosions that seemed to last several minutes. Soon after this ceased, I heard someone groaning and gasping to breathe. Getting out of the dugout, I found one of my AB's doubled over and holding his stomach. It was a chap named Menheniott, who was one of the lads dug into the footings of where the bungalow had been demolished. I got him into our dugout, and after a while realised that he had no visible injuries, but had had all the breath knocked out of him. When thinking, as I did, that the bomb was a delay, he had put his head out of his shelter and it was then that it exploded, causing his shelter to collapse on him when he was half way out.

Eventually he recovered his breath, then said 'Tuck Sir'; I said 'what's wrong with Tuck?' 'He's buried in the shelter,' he managed to say. I ran over to where their shelter was located, still in my socks, shirt and trousers, and started pulling sandbags and pieces of timber from the collapsed roof of the shelter. I then spotted a couple more lads emerge from a hole at the other end of the footings. I called out to them to give me a hand; it was quite dark and I had no idea who they were. They just set to, and we moved a fair amount of debris when one of the lads said, 'who's in here Sir?' 'Tuck,' I replied; 'No I aint,' he said. 'I was in the other hole.'

Fortunately, no one was seriously hurt; Menheniott was taken to a field hospital before being shipped home to make a full recovery. I learned later that he achieved a commission. The many small explosions that we heard after the initial bomb blast were caused by the clods of earth falling on the 'Shoe' mines, causing most of them explode harmlessly.

Some little while after this incident, we managed to get hold of some salt-water soap for general usage. Bob Campbell and I were sharing a watch on the beach; it was high water and craft movements had been completed, so I suggested to Bob that he take his lads into the water for general bathing for half an hour, then I would follow with the remainder when they had completed their bathing session. It was my luck to be in the water when the PBM happened along, and to receive a rollocking for treating this as a seaside holiday.

I bit my tongue until my period of duty finished, and then went along to see him. 'I suppose you have come along to apologise,' he said. 'No Sir,' I replied, 'I have come to complain re. your conduct toward me in front of the ratings, as you did not ask why we were in the water'. I then explained that we had been on the beach for two months without the facilities for bathing, and that I had managed to get hold of some salt-water soap so that we could freshen up. Also that we had not left the beach unattended at any time, as midshipman Campbell had bathed with his section first whilst I covered, and that I had only just entered the water with my lads when he arrived on the scene. I got my apology, also his approval for further bathing when circumstances allowed.

We seemed to get along quite well after that little spat, and a couple of days later he asked me to take over 'J1' party, as lieutenant Bill Lindsay had been transferred to the NOIC's staff. It was to be a temporary posting. Furthermore, I was to go onto ITEM RED Beach to ensure the safe beaching of the MARK V LCTs. These craft were longer than the general run of LCTs, as they had been constructed to carry the *Queen-Mary* Long Loader Air-Craft Transporters of the RAF recovery Units. Their extra length made them vulnerable to breaking their backs should they lie on any beach that was other than flat. ITEM RED Beach at Le Hamel had a number of areas that could accommodate them.

I was sorry to leave my little dug-out and the lads of 'J2', also our two cooks in their nearby galley. But then life is full of changes, and I was quite happy to see that the leading seaman who came to drive me to the other beach in a Jeep was my old corporal from my days in the home guard back in South Benfleet. We arrived outside the front of a house which was somewhat damaged by shelling; the upper floors were still habitable, and this is where I found my new team, especially one able seaman Brown. He was a large, friendly giant, who had found some furnishings, beds, carpets and chairs to make it a very comfortable billet. I had a small room overlooking the sea and the beaches that we were going to work. The house had probably been used as a guesthouse prior to the war. The other lads were happily settled in the remainder of the building.

I was quite happy to remain in those quarters, as the control office shared by the Army and myself was situated in the house next door but one. It was too good to last; just two weeks later the Army declared the buildings unsafe, and put in the bulldozers. It was soon after arriving on ITEM RED Beach that I had a visit from my old shipmate Jimmy Jewiss. He came into the control office one afternoon, much to my surprise, so we had a lot of catching up to do. I learned from him that the rest of my old flotilla were on ITEM GREEN Beach, so I took time off when I had a quiet spell to go and see them.

I met my old CO Lt Russell Smith, who said that he had been following my progress and wished me well. I met a few more of my old flotilla comrades, and was pleased to learn that they all were in good spirits, and very helpful with supplies of fuel from the LBO for my LCP, that I had won. In fact, when we returned to the UK, I left it in their charge, it being of great use to them whilst in Arromanches.

On moving from the now-demolished houses in Le Hamel, we took over some space on the upper floor of the sanatorium, where we had a superb view of the beaches and the many LCT's laying up ready to discharge their loads. It was easy to keep in touch with them with the aldis lamp, especially on one occasion when I had the report of a hospital ship being torpedoed by a midget submarine off the

LBO (foreground), LBK (left), and LBE (right), with smaller craft; small Admiral's barge taking HM King George VI ashore.

beachhead. All bar one was under way within minutes; the odd one had problems with his engines.

I had found a comfortable place to sleep in a large air-raid shelter that was stocked with hundreds of bottles of vichy water, though I did not like the taste, so it was still there when I left. I had located a camp-bed and folding chair; these, together with a couple of empty compo ration boxes for stowage purposes, meant I was quite comfortable.

For lighting purposes, we used an empty flat sweet tin, about an inch deep by three inches wide, and five inches in length. A small hole was punched through the center of the lid and a wick of canvas or other suitable material inserted through it, leaving about a quarter of an inch exposed; the tin was then half filled with sand. When topped up with petrol, this would burn for hours with a clear candle-bright light. Something I believe the Desert Rats invented in the Western Desert. It certainly worked well for me until a certain day in August.

This was the day when I celebrated my twenty-first birthday, or, nearly didn't. On 15 August, the first spirit ration was distributed to the naval lads on the beach. The officers had the choice of a bottle of whisky or gin; I chose the whisky, and put it aside for later consumption. On that particular day I was joined by Ronnie Wheeler, the Lieutenant in charge of 'J3', who was now surplus due to the phoenix piers running so well in Arromanches; so he came along to give me a spell on ITEM RED Beach.

We were still covering the look-out on the upper floor at 11.00 p.m. when Ron mentioned that it was my birthday coming up, and that we should celebrate it with a toast, suggesting that I get my bottle out. At 12.30, having passed the bottle round to a number of people who were in the control room, and whose only drinking vessels were enamel mugs, my bottle looked decidedly empty. 'I think it is your turn now Ron,' I said, to which he agreed.

I don't remember getting to bed, but that's where I was when my leading seaman woke me the next morning to take me along to ITEM GREEN Beach to collect the rum rations for my lads. Lt-Com. Bell and Tom Hewitt were there to supervise this issue, but not before insisting that I have a wee dram; before I could get away quite a lot of the lads offered me sippers of their rum. I had reached my limit, and frankly I was feeling a little bit under the weather. I cannot remember if I had any food that day, and when I arrived back on my beach, Ronnie Wheeler said 'it's my watch, you turn in for a while'. I did not argue and went down to my camp-bed and crashed out.

It must have been about 6.00 a.m. when I woke up. My little spirit lamp was out, so I decided to top it up with petrol from a half empty Jerry can that I had nearby. I must have spilled a little, or had not put the lid on securely, for when I lit the wick the whole lot flared up, engulfing the sleeves of my battle dress. I was fortunate that my blanket was on my bed and close to me; I swiftly wrapped this round my arms and doused the flames at the same time. I must have been born under a lucky star. Not only had I survived, I did not even suffer any burns or singeing to hair or eyebrows. It was the most efficient sobering remedy I have ever experienced.

I am not sure now whether it was in that week or the week before when we watched the first thousand Bombers Raid over Caen. This town had held out since D-Day, with very heavy resistance by the Germans. The day prior to the raid we witnessed a flying fortress shot down over the beach head; we could see a wing fall away, and then saw seven parachutes leave the plane before it crashed and exploded some distance away.

The parachutes began to drift inland toward Caen, and then we noticed anti-aircraft shells exploding around the unfortunate and defenseless airmen. We were hopping mad, so the next day when we saw the bombs rain down on Caen, we cheered our heads off. As the aircraft flew over our heads, they were flashing the 'V' sign to us below. A few days later, I witnessed thousands of German prisoners-of-war being marched down to the beach by British 'Tommies'; it was a wonderful sight.

The following week, in fact seven days after my twenty-first birthday, we were on a ship homeward bound. It was LSI landing ship *Ulster Monarch*, formally a ferry between Belfast and the UK, now fitted out as troop ship with LCAs slung from her davits instead of life-boats. I had at least one of my prayers answered; I went to France as a twenty year old, and reached my maturity in more ways than one. I guess I could say that I had grown up and left boyhood far behind.

It was a comfortable trip back to Portsmouth; my only grumble was the fact that the only drink that was served on board was Guinness; oh, what I wouldn't have given for a Mann's Brown Ale. We were allowed six pints each; I gave up after the first two, which considering the effect they had on me later was a wise decision. We disembarked in Portsmouth the following morning, and were entrained up to Waterloo Station, arriving somewhere around noon. Here food was laid on for the lads at the Union Jack Club. We were there for a couple of hours before being taken across London by troop carriers to Euston Station; here we boarded a train for the North, but not before the sirens heralded another night of bombing, something we had forgotten about whilst in Normandy.

The journey north was a long and tiring one; the compartment reserved for the officers was in the middle section of a carriage. I was about midway between the toilets that, after battling through crowded corridors, always appeared to be engaged, which was unfortunate as those couple of pints of Guinness started to have their effect on me. Perhaps it was due to the change of diet; after all, we had been living on compo rations for nearly four months, and perhaps there was some truth in that rumour about putting something in our food to stop us following our natural instincts. I wasn't very regular in Normandy, but I certainly made up for it on that journey north. We arrived at Waverley Station, Edinburgh, in time for breakfast; the lads had this laid on for them at nearby canteen, whilst the officers were invited to take theirs in the Great Northern Hotel.

We had a quick wash and brush up in the cloak room before making our way into the dining room, where we were met by the maître d', who earnestly requested us to leave our weapons outside the door in case they offended the other guests. We had been so used to wearing them that they had become part of our every-day life. Having humoured him by placing them in a corner where we could keep a watchful eye on them, we enjoyed a breakfast of sausage, powdered egg, beans and toast with a nice pot of tea. It was all served with nice clean linen tablecloths and napkins; this was decidedly better than the way we felt. The bathtubs at Hopetoun were beckoning, where we would enjoy a good long soak, and then change into our blue uniforms.

We were given a great welcome when we arrived back. Arrangements were made for payment to the lads, and leave was granted for fourteen days on the next morning. I did have one upset when a Customs and Excise man turned up, demanding that the lads could only take 100 cigarettes home with them, as we had been missed when we landed in Portsmouth. I could not get over this, and went to see him to ask how he would have liked to have spent nearly four months on the beaches, with just six cigarettes a day rationed, to then have someone like him come along and say you are only entitled to a paltry fifty cigarettes that were purchased from the NAAFI canteen, and were not even duty free. I think he took my point and left.

I, unfortunately, was in no position to travel for another four days, until my stomach settled down. I eventually arrived home to find the house empty; both my parents were working, dad was in the Woolwich Arsenal, and my mother in a nearby factory where she was engaged as an oxy-acetylene welder on tank parts; she had done welding in the First World War. I had been unable to tell either of them that I was coming home as we had no telephone at home, and I did not wish to send a telegram as normally they only conveyed news of casualties, and I did not wish to shock them.

I went into my local, the Papermakers Arms, just across the road from the factory where mum worked – I knew that some of

Jack Gaster with his father, Joe, February 1944.

her workmates would be in there at lunch-time. They soon let her know I was there; she did not even stop to take off her leather apron and goggles from her forehead, but came running over to give me one of the biggest hugs I have ever experienced. It was good to be home, and though my local did not sell Mann's Brown, the beer that Charrington's brewed was a very good substitute.

It was good to be home, though the nights often had to be spent in the air raid shelter in the park. I did try sleeping in my room, but it worried my mother so much that I had to give in a few times. There were quite a number of empty spaces amongst the rows of houses where bombs had taken their toll, rather like missing teeth in a set of dentures. I contacted Waterman's Hall whilst I was home to see about obtaining my Freedom, having nearly finished my seven years apprenticeship. I was delighted to learn that the sittings for the granting of licenses and freedoms would be held in September, on the second Tuesday in the month, a date four days after my leave was up. I sent a telegram off to my commanding officer explaining the reason why I wanted an extension of leave, and was pleased to receive confirmation by telegram the following day.

I attended the Hall in uniform, where I met many more apprentices who were finishing their time, to find that most were in uniforms, covering nearly every branch of the armed forces. I had to explain that I had not seen my Master since the early days of the Blitz. That appeared to be no problem, as my uniform showed that I had become worthy to become a Freeman of the Company of Watermen and Lightermen of the River Thames.

On leaving the Hall after the traditional jug of ale had been passed around, I made my way over to Rotherhithe to see my old bosses; they were delighted to see me, and Dave Hawkins, the first tug skipper that I worked with and now the manager of the company, took me round to see the little tug *Hawk*, now sporting a new and more powerful engine. My leave was over all too soon, and on returning to Hopetoun I had to produce my licenses and Freedom Certificate to my CO, where upon I was congratulated and treated to a few drinks by members of the commando.

It was not long after this that we were on the move again back to *Armadillo*, where we had a good reception and enjoyed watching some new lads put through their paces, not that we were allowed to sit back and take it easy. We still had to keep our lads fit, and were back into the old routine of route marches, cross-country runs, though in that location it was more climbing than running; though it is funny that most of our runs ended in the Whistlefield Inn on the road to Inveraray, a distance of twelve miles or so. It was not unusual for us after an evening in Dunoon, where the little MFV liberty boat that we had at *Armadillo* would convey us for our run ashore and an evenings dancing at the Pavilion, for us to miss the return run and walk the fifteen to sixteen miles back to Ardentinny. We were always made welcome in that community, it was like coming home whenever we were there.

On leaving there at the beginning of October, we were shipped down the loch to Gourock, but not before the lads had decorated the flag post on the little pier with a signal halyard full of assorted ladies underwear, mostly they were navy blue, with just a few of khaki. On arrival at our destination, which proved to be Coalhouse Fort at East Tilbury on the River Thames (the scene of my entanglement with that under water cable just two and a half years before, was it just that short time ago?), an urgent signal reached us to ask if the 'S' mine that was left on the armory table by some person who shall remain nameless had been made safe. No one would go near it. As the Commando detrained at East Tilbury Station, I was called on to march them to the Fort; this was a distance of one mile. As we approached the Fort, I called on them to march to attention to pass through the gate where a Royal Marine Sentry presented arms; as I returned his salute I was surprised to see it was my cousin.

It was like stepping back a couple centuries inside the Fort, built to stop the fleets of Napoleon and of the Dutch from raiding our Ports and this country. The old gun emplacements were there, but without the cannons of the eighteenth and nineteenth century. Instead, mounted on the top of the deep-walled enclosure, were two eight inch guns manned by the Royal Maritime Artillery, covering the Lower Hope and Sea Reaches of the Thames to prevent any incursions from enemy vessels into the upper reaches.

As soon as my cousin, Frank Gaster, was relieved of his sentry duty on the gate we had a good long chat. It would appear that he had spent a long time out in the Middle East and the Red Sea area, where he had met my uncle Henry, who was a CSM with a Royal Engineers Port Operating Group, in charge of a 'Z' Craft, something I believe about the size of a tank landing craft. Frank was doubly related; his mother and my mother were sisters, and his father was my father's first cousin. His younger brother Leonard had lost a leg whilst mine-sweeping off Singapore prior to the Japanese invasions in that area; their youngest brother Leslie was engaged in mine sweepers in the North Sea, so you can see that with a few exceptions, we were a family of sailors, including our 'marine' or 'Bootneck' as naval terminology has it.

Frank lived in Pitsea, so this was almost a home posting for him, whilst I was only a matter of five stations away from Barking, and a short bus ride from my home. Needless to say, I took every opportunity to take native leave and usually invited one of my fellow officers home with me for a stopover. One was Bobby Campbell, who stayed on a couple of occasions; I think he was a little taken with my younger sister Irene who, being a cockney like me, had a job to understand Bob's broad Yorkshire accent.

Phil Cockshoot, who was a Sub-Lieutenant RNVR, and was the replacement for Bill Stephens in 'J3' when he was promoted to Lieutenant in charge of 'J2', accompanied me one evening, and whilst we were having a quiet drink in the Papermakers, our friendly barmaid said that if we fancied going to a dance, there was one being held in the Guild Hall of the Catholic Church in the Ilford High Road. As we had nothing better to do, we made our way along to the Hall where we were made very welcome. It was a friendly place and we soon found dancing partners. I had just seen the young lady who I had danced with back to her seat when my eyes caught those of a rather beautiful blonde, curly-headed young lady who had just arrived with another girl. Do not ask me what her friend looked like as I only had eyes for my vision of loveliness. I was smitten, and had to reach her before any one else could rob me of the chance to speak to her. I asked her if she would like this dance that had just been announced, and to my utter delight, my offer was accepted.

Phil Cockshoot danced with her friend. I suppose that you could say that I monopolised the rest of the evening with her. When the interval was announced, we asked our lovely partners if they would like to have a drink with us. As drinks were not permitted on the premises, it meant a short walk across the High Street to the nearest public house, the Earl Hainault; the girls only had ciders whilst we had a couple of halves of brown ale. I should have mentioned Phill's parents owned a pub, The Blue Cap Inn, up in Chester.

We returned to the hall a happy and cheerful party, and were sorry to hear the announcement for the last waltz. I did not want to lose contact with this young lady, whose name, I learned, was Phyllis Francis – a beautiful name for a beautiful girl. As we left the hall the sirens sounded their mournful dirge; we could expect the worst. This was when the V1s or doodle-bugs had become a menace in the south-east of England. I saw Phyllis to her trolley-bus; she lived some four miles out at Barkingside. I would have loved to have accompanied her except that I had the responsibility of getting Phil Cockshoot back home to my place as he had no idea where he was. Also, we were on parade for divisions in the morning.

I did get the promise of a date later on, so I went home happy. I was even happier when I found that we had a supper of bread and cheese with fresh pickled shallots that my father had just bottled. We soon had a change of leadership when Lt-Com. Bell left the commando, to be replaced by a Lt-Com. Peter Eggerton, a very interesting man who had once had command of a MTB Flotilla in the English Channel. Bill Stephens left on medical grounds, and two Lieutenants RNVR arrived to take over the vacant beachmasters positions for 'J1' and 'J2' parties, apparently some of the commandos were being disbanded now that the Normandy landings had been accomplished. 'J' Commando was to be held in reserve. I suppose that I was a little disappointed not to have been rated up to Lieutenant and confirmed as beachmaster with 'J1' or 'J2', but I suppose I was only just turned twenty-one, and had less than eighteen months seniority in my rank.

We still kept our regular training exercises and route march going, getting to know the area very well. The home guard battalion at Stanford-le-Hope were running down their collection of explosives that had been held in the anticipation of any attempted invasion by Germany. They had seen our lads out training on a few occasions and thought we could find use for such items.

Tom Hewitt, Ronnie Wheeler, petty officer Fedder and myself went along to their armoury to see what they had to offer, and to see what condition it was in. We were met by a regular army staff sergeant, who conducted us to a nearby chalk quarry where it was situated. It was decided that we should test some of the explosives, so we all took a few samples to try out in the quarry. I had a coil of cortex instantaneous fuse draped over my arm, some dry guncotton and a box of fuses carried in the other; the others were all similarly laden. The staff sergeant then decided to show us his prize possessions, some bakelite hand grenades, something we had used many times; however we thought we could afford to humour him as he was our host. 'You unscrew this cap like this, then as you throw it, the tape with this lead pellet on the end, unwinds and pulls the pin just like this.' As he said these words, he put back his arm and threw the grenade; unfortunately for all of us he was standing on some loose chalk, which crumbled under his foot just as he was about to let fly.

The grenade went upward instead of away, and landed just a couple of feet from us. For one frozen second we watched in horror, then we dispersed in all directions in the hope that we could be far enough away when it exploded – nothing happened, we didn't know whether it was a dud or a delayed action. Leaving our motley collection at a safe distance, we approached the unexploded grenade, and then we could see that the pin had only been pulled half out because of the shortened flight. It was too tricky to touch, so we put a detonator with a slow fuse as close to it as we dared, thus giving ourselves ample time to walk far enough away to a safe distance.

Thankfully, when it did explode we were still in one piece. They were not particularly deadly, but when you are laden with sensitive explosives at that short distance anything could have happened. It was not long after this incident that the commando was invited to take part in an Armistice Day parade at East Tilbury, where the Bata Shoe factory was situated. A little community had sprung up, with houses and a parade of shops with a large parking area to the front.

It was decided that I would be the officer in charge of the guard of honour. So all the riflemen from 'J' commando, with belts, gaiters, and rifle slings whitened, fell in to be marched from the fort – after being inspected by the CO – to the position where the parade was to be held. We were joined by a sea cadet band who led the way from the fort and played reasonably well, but who lacked a full marching pace so that we had to shorten step a few times to avoid treading on their heels.

I had the lads marching to attention in column of route so that very few orders were necessary; we right wheeled onto the parade area following the band, who were supposed to turn left along the parade area, then left again at the far end where we would come to a halt. They turned left as agreed, then almost immediately counter marched across the approaching guard. I just had time to call 'mark time' then forward, as they once again counter marched from our path. All went well after that and the lads put up a good show. We then had to march back to a little church near to the fort, where we were received by the local priest with a choking for being late in the house of God. I think that we should have led the parade with the band running after us.

I managed to get home a few times to renew my acquaintance with my heart's desire, a walk in the local park on a Sunday, the odd visits to the dance hall – I really enjoyed this – then one evening she told me her father had managed to get home on a twenty-four hour leave. He was a flight sergeant engineer in Lancasters; I was very pleased to meet him and Phyllis's mother. They were of Welsh stock, but had lived in the London area for a number of years. In fact, her father had been the chief air-raid warden in Barkingside for a number of years before feeling that he needed to hit back by joining the Air Force.

We decided to have a drink in the local pub, where I failed to ingratiate myself with her father. On asking him to have a drink, he decided on a bitter and I had my usual brown and mild. The barman produced a half of bitter, and of course the brown and mild was a half of each, making a pint. I tried to remedy the situation, feeling a little embarrassed but I need not have worried. He saw the funny side of the situation. I did make up for it, however, when I agreed to collect a bike that he borrowed to get to Ilford Station in order to catch an early train, and return it to the owner. He showed me some of the aerial photos of places they had targeted along the Rhine; he was with a Pathfinder Squadron, a job that required a lot of courage and nerves of steel. Sadly, we were never to meet again, he was posted missing the following February.

Whilst I was at Tilbury, an old school friend of mine called on my mother to say that he was on leave, having just got home from France, and that he was celebrating his twenty-first birthday at home with a party and that he would like me to be there. This was back in my old hometown, in Burdett Road. I asked Phyllis if she would care to go with me, to which she readily agreed. I know that I should not have done, but after seeing squaddies parading about wearing their green berets and the red berets of the Paras, I thought it was about time we showed them that the Navy had its own Special Forces. I wore my Khaki uniform with white belt and gaiters; I think Phyllis did not like it as much as my blue uniform. The party was a bit of a disappointment, as after a very short stay at his house we adjourned to the local where my friend and I used to play darts; immediately we were asked to have a game. Normally I was not a very good player, but that night, every time I threw a dart, it was a winner.

We just could not lose, and every time we won a game, a pint was put on the counter for us. Remember this was where I grew up, and I was known to all the people there that night; poor Phyllis was amongst strangers, though I am sure they made her welcome. When my friend Con Emmerman finished playing, the bar was filled with pints of beer from one end to the other, and we were made to finish them before leaving. I can remember leaving the pub, The Earl of Zetland, and boarding a number 25 bus from Mile End Station to go to Ilford, but my memory lapsed after that.

I must have got home safely, but could not remember how or when I was supposed to see Phyllis again. I know, I thought, I'll go to Ilford Station, where we usually met when she finished work, at the usual time and take a chance. This time I was wearing my blue uniform; sure enough, she came into the station, a little startled to see me there, and immediately grabbed my arm and walked me out of the station and along the road. 'I did not expect to see you there,' she said, 'in fact I wasn't going to see you again'.

Apparently she had decided to meet some one else, but rather than cause a scene, led me away as soon as she could before her date turned up. 'I don't think I have ever been so embarrassed,' she said, then went on to explain that when we got on the bus at Mile End, there was only one seat, the side seat by the stairs and no room on top. I made her take the seat, then I stood under the stairway so that I was leaning over her and, after paying the fare, I began by asking her to marry me, not once but many times. 'When are you going to marry me? Will you marry me', and so on until by the time the bus reached Manor Park some ten or more miles further on, the conductor said 'For Gawd's sake say yes, and give us all a bit of Peace'. I could understand her coolness, but it did not change my mind. So I said 'I am stone cold sober now and I still want to marry you.'

It was my turn to leave the commando now; I had heard that Bill Tewsley had joined the tug service, and I was feeling ready for a change so I asked Peter Eggerton if he would mind if I put in for a transfer; not at all, he said, you will get a good reference from me, so I put in a request for Sea Rescue and Salvage work, giving my previous experience in tugs etc. hoping that I might be considered. Almost by return I received a signal to report to Fanum House, an annexe of the Admiralty, where I was to report to Captain Thompson RNR, the officer commanding the Rescue Tug Service of the Royal Navy.

I thought that perhaps my pre-service work as an apprentice waterman and lighterman, which was mainly spent in towage work, would be to my advantage. As I have mentioned, I obtained my Freedom in the September of 1944, on my return from France, and was now fully fledged as a waterman and lighterman.

So on a wintry Friday morning, decked out in my best 'Blues', I was admitted into the presence of Captain Thompson, RNR, where I was to sign articles as a second officer T.124T. This, I was later to learn, was the Auxiliary Tug Service that had been under the Navy's wing, and now proudly flew the White Ensign whilst engaged on its services to the Allied Fleets, assisting them to make port with their precious cargoes. My rank was to be the same Sub-Lieutenant; RNVR with the added T.124T, which signified I was under Board of Trade articles of the Rescue Tug Service.

CHAPTER NINE

# ENIGMA

I was somewhat surprised to learn that not only had I been accepted for the tug service, but that I was expected to join my vessel at Harwich on the following Monday. I asked if I might be allowed to take a refresher course in navigation, as the last time I had received any instructions in this art had been when I was on my commissioning course at Loch Ailort in August and September of 1943, and since then I had been more of a 'soldier' than a sailor whilst with the commandos.

I was politely informed by Captain Thompson that I would have to make application after joining my ship at Harwich, and no doubt this could be arranged for at a future date – I still had not attended a refresher course when I was finally paid off in March 1947 at Parkestone Quay, by which time I thought, and felt, that I could cope with anything. I had received some practical tuition from two years or more of towing and salvage work that carried me halfway round the world and back.

On the Saturday morning I took a somewhat drunken leave of the wardroom at Colehouse Fort, and of my Commanding officer, Lt-Com. Peter Eggerton, at the Orsett Cock P.H., near Grays, Essex. I had said goodbye to Combined Ops., and had started a new phase in my service with the Navy.

I spent a pleasant Saturday evening and Sunday morning at my home with my folks and the girl who was later to become my wife, and then caught the afternoon train from Ilford to Harwich, where I was to report to Lt-Com. Green, RNR, the senior officer rescue tugs at Harwich. The headquarters at Harwich were situated in the Great Eastern Hotel. Here I was given a meal and a 'cabin' for the night, and was informed that the *Enigma* (the tug that I was to join) was out on a rescue job, and was not expected back until the morning.

Since leaving the comfort of the wardroom at Colehouse Fort, I had been turning over in my mind as to what type of tug the *Enigma* was. I had obviously seen most of the 'Biguns' on the Thames, but even on the biggest of these a second Officer would only be a glorified 'deck-hand'. I could visualise myself throwing heavy lines, heaving on tow-ropes and taking the occasional turn at the wheel. Little did I know what was in store for me, or how soon I was to be in for a really big surprise.

At about 8.30 p.m. that evening I had eaten, and my time was my own till morning, so I decided to 'wet my whistle' in the Pier Hotel next door. It was rather dead for a pub, and after having a couple, I was on the point of leaving, when in through the door walked a Sub-Lieutenant (E) RNVR. We acknowledged each other, and were soon engaged in friendly conversation.

He asked what ship I was from, and when I replied that I was waiting to join, 'Not the *Enigma*?' I was somewhat taken aback, and replied in the affirmative. He shook hands and said, 'Welcome aboard, we're just in.' I immediately said, 'I suppose you are the Chief Engineer?' To which he grinned, 'No, I'm Nobby the third'. Again I was shaken. 'What kind of ship was the *Enigma*?' 'Would you like to have a look at her?' he asked. I could not suppress my curiosity, and so we left the pub together and crossed the road to the pier, where I espied a boat moored to the steps; it was about twenty-seven feet by about eight, and powered by a petrol paraffin engine.

I asked if this was loaned to them whilst in harbour; when he told me it was the ship's boat I really began to wonder what size the tug was, and some ten minutes later we slid under the stern, and alongside the biggest tug I have ever seen, or could have imagined. In the dark she looked huge, but when I climbed over the ladder and stood on the afterdeck she looked gigantic.

Looking up onto the afterend of the boat deck, I could see the barrel of a 12-pounder gun pointing aft, and beyond a mizzen mast that towered some sixty feet into the night sky. Alongside of me, flaked out on the deck, was a towrope as big as a man's thigh, eighteen inches in circumference and one hundred and twenty fathoms in length, to which was shackled a sixty-fathom, six-inch wire rope. Thinking back to the towropes I had used on the Thames, you could imagine my feelings.

I followed Nobby forward beneath the boat deck, along a sheltered area measuring some twenty feet by ten; through a door on my left I could see down into the depths of the boiler room, where two giant oil-fired boilers dwarfed a stoker who was busy tending to some valves far below.

We stepped through a doorway in the bulkhead running across the ship into an alleyway that led forward, on the outside of which was situated the officers' bathroom and shower room. Beyond this was a companion way leading up to the boat deck, emerging first below the starboard wing of the bridge. On our left was another entrance to the boiler room, and immediately forward of this a fair sized galley with its gleaming pots and pans and a large oil-fired range. Nobby took pride in showing me an emergency escape hatch that led up from the mess decks below, up through a shaft emerging through a door each side of the bottom leading into the seamens' and firemens' messes respectively.

Forward of the galley was a small wardroom pantry, and the wardroom itself. The wardroom measured some fifteen by ten feet; there were two tables, with places for four at each table, a couple of easy chairs and small bar. The alleyway went around the wardroom on three sides; on the outer side were situated the cabins and petty officers' mess.

My cabin (I was later to discover) was on the port side immediately below the boat deck and opposite the bathroom on the other side of the ship. I was right over the boiler room, so had little need for the radiator in my cabin. I was happy later on to change this for the 'pilot's' cabin below the bridge when I learned we were going to the tropics, but this was to be nearly ten months later.

I was introduced to some of the other members of the wardroom: Sid Hewitt, an RNR S/Lt, ex-Humber Trinity House and 1st Mate of the *Enigma*; Ronnie Knight an RNVR S/Lt (E) Chief Engineer, and 'Mac' (McConnell the 2nd Radio officer). They were a friendly

'The crazy gang' March 1945.

crowd and I soon felt at home with them. After a couple of 'Tots' Sid Hewitt said, 'I suppose we had better introduce you to the "old man".' I followed him up the companionway, emerging onto the boatdeck opposite a rather impressive radio room. From there by ladder up on to the wing of the bridge, where an Orlikon gun was situated; the *Enigma* had one on each wing of the bridge, and up on the flying bridge or 'Monkey Island' were twin mountings, each containing a pair of .5 Browning machine guns. Whatever else, we certainly weren't short of armament.

As we stepped into the darkened wheelhouse, I could see brasswork gleaming everywhere; from the shaded red light over the chart table in the far corner, everywhere was spotlessly clean, and I felt a pride in the ship.

Sid drew aside a blackout curtain, and we stepped through into a chart room immediately behind the wheelhouse; there he knocked on a door on the far side. a few seconds elapsed before a voice bid us enter, and I was face to face with a large red faced fairheaded man with bristly eyebrows. I had met my new Captain, Lt Brice, RNR MBE.

For a few seconds he studied me, and then asked me what service I had, and whether I had any navigational experience. He did not appear to be very impressed with my answers, and I began to view my immediate future with apprehension, but I need not have worried. I had a good mate and tutor in the person of Sid who showed me the ropes in more ways than one.

My first fleeting visit on board the *Enigma* had left me with a mixed feeling of pride and awe. I went to bed that night in my temporary quarters ashore, but it was some time before sleep came. My mind was full of what I had seen, and I began to wonder if maybe I had taken on more than I had bargained for. Eventually I fell sound asleep, and awoke in the morning well before time. I hastily had a shower and packed my overnight things, enjoyed a good breakfast and reported as soon as the senior officer rescue tugs office was open, so that I could board *Enigma* by the first available boat.

I was somewhat surprised to learn that the *Enigma* was no longer at her mooring, and the transport that would convey me to her was in fact a car.

She had been called out soon after I had come ashore, to go to the assistance of SS *Sam York*, a 10,000 ton 'liberty' ship that had gone

Painting of HMS *Enigma* W175.

aground on the 'Hammond Knoll', a sand bank on the Norfolk coast. During this operation her screw had fouled the 'messenger' rope as the wire hawser was being passed from the tug's stern to the ship, and before anything could be done to stop engines, she had wound the wire around the screw.

The anchor was immediately let go, but the severity of heavy swells that were running parted the anchor cable, and *Enigma* was driven towards the 'Knoll' herself and was in grave danger of broaching. The Skipper decided to make the best speed he could into Yarmouth. The effort proved to be costly for *Enigma*; as she entered a berth alongside Yarmouth Quay, her tail end shaft seized solid.

I joined *Enigma* at 11.00 a.m. Shortly after my arrival, an Admiralty diver arrived and went overside to inspect the damage. The report he gave did not take very much time: *Enigma* was to be dry-docked.

Early next morning, the United Towing Company Tug *Kruman* arrived to take us in tow to Immingham. I thought I could detect a slightly superior smile on the faces of her crew, and some of our lads who had previously worked for 'United' looked a bit sheepish.

The tow up to the Humber went without any trouble; one could almost say peacefully, as so many of the crew were able to catch up on lost sleep. We arrived at Immingham on the following afternoon's tide, and were expertly manoeuvred into the dry dock by a couple of the docking tugs.

The following day leave was granted to half the ship's company; this was to include Christmas and Boxing Day. The remainder, of which I was a part, were to be home for the New Year.

Those of us who remained on board over Christmas had quite a good time; there were a number of 'Sweepers' in dock, and invitations were had from all sides to celebrate the holiday. We were also joined by a Danish Collier, and Christmas and Boxing Day became something of a hazy recollection.

That winter was very severe. *Enigma* with her boilers blown down was like an ice-box; extra blankets were issued to all on board.

At the beginning of February repairs were completed, trials were over and *Enigma* was once more ready for sea. Everyone on board had enjoyed either Christmas or New Year at home, and we were now busy settling down to ship's routine.

The day arrived for us to set sail back to Harwich; at 11.00 a.m. we cleared the lock, and set course down stream. Spurn Point was cleared at midday when I reported to the bridge for my first sea-going watch.

Alas, I did not get off to a very good start; the skipper called me over to the wing of the bridge and gave me a lecture on the size of my 'wine' bill. I tried to explain that we had entertained a lot of people on board during our stay in dry dock, and that as *Enigma* had been a cold ship something warm was needed inside. He thought that a 'bottle a day' was just a bit too much!

I was in the middle of my apologies when he suddenly gave the helmsman an order to come ten degrees to starboard. His next words were directed at me, and took me somewhat by surprise, 'Con the Ship', he said. I must have looked as dumb as I felt, as his next few words were quite a bit more colourful, as were my ears. Eventually I began to realise that I was required to climb up onto the 'Monkey island', steady the course down on the top compass and give any corrections required to the man at the wheel.

The remainder of that watch I was up and down like a 'Yo-Yo', taking bearings of everything that moved or didn't move, checking the chart, checking the course, checking the speed. I was not going to be caught out again. The two ABs with whom I shared my watch must have thought I had St Vitus' dance. I think they were suffering from the cold from the amount of cocoa they were drinking, or it could have been the draught I caused every time I was in and out of the wheelhouse.

At 4.00 p.m. Sid Hewitt, the mate, came up onto the bridge. I gave him a detailed account of our position, course steered, other vessels in the vicinity, and anything and everything else I could think of. He just looked at me and grinned. 'Don't worry lad, get down to the wardroom before it's all gone,' he said, and added, 'It looks as though you have earned it.' Feeling a little better, I made my way below.

My first watch was over and *Enigma* was still afloat, and what's more, pointed in the right direction; life wasn't so bad after all. We arrived at Harwich the next morning and made fast to the buoys off Shotley Point. the ship's company then settled down to normal routine that required an hour's notice for steam. Leave was granted on the understanding that no one went further than Harwich, and that in the event of the recal signal of 'W' sounded on the ship's whistle, they would return with all haste to the pier. The local cinema had a special slide for rescue tug personnel to return to ship. This would be shown by an arrangement of the senior officer rescue tugs office at Harwich.

The 'Local' for the rescue tug personnel at Harwich was The Three Cups, and many a happy hour was spent in the little private bar at the rear of those premises. Nelson and Lady Hamilton were reputed to have stayed there in the days of yore; quite frankly, I was inclined to believe they shared the same decorations by the look of the place. However, the Lady of the House and her two charming daughters made up for the drabness of the place. A lot of time was spent in their company, and they on their part adopted the rescue tug lads as their own.

A week or two after our return to Harwich, we had our first 'job'; a 5,000 ton collier, the *Empire Seaman,* had gone aground on the south side of the Edinburgh Channel on top of a spring tide. As soon as we arrived we got a line on board using our 'Schermully' (Thames for the use of) Rocket, and soon connected up the tow. We pulled her head round about fifteen degrees, but that was as far as she would budge – a wall of sand had built up along her side.

The next morning's tide was the last of the 'springs', and an all-out effort was planned. We were joined by the ex-French tug *Champion* (now flying the White Ensign) and a couple of 'Sun' tugs, together with the old PLA salvage vessel *Yanlet*. An hour before high water, with the tow connected, we began the operation. The skipper was using the strong flood tide to give weight to the pull by allowing his head to fall away, and then lever back against the pressure of tide against *Enigma's* starboard bow.

The rope was leading out over our starboard side across to the bows of the Collier, where it was led in through a hawsehole right up in the bows, and then back to her mooring bitts on the port bow. As the additional strain came onto the tow-rope, it would lift clear of water; this would take some doing normally, as a rope of one hundred and twenty fathoms together with some sixty fathoms of 6 inch wire required a tremendous strain to lift in normal circumstances.

For about half an hour this operation was repeated, then, perhaps by design or because of some extra weight of tide, our head fell away to port so that we were almost abreast of the tide. The Skipper gave a double ring ahead on the telegraph for emergency power ahead, and brought the wheel hard to starboard.

*Enigma* laid well over on her side as she answered to the increased thrust from her large screw. Her boat deck on the starboard side was coming down to meet the water, the tow-rope pulled straight, the sea water being squeezed from every fibre, was beginning to vibrate with the strain; then we began to move, and I thought we had won, but looking across to the bows of the *Empire Seaman* I saw a sight that I doubt I shall ever see again.

The 6 inch wire was no longer leading in at the bow; in fact, it was cutting its way through the metal of her forward plates like the wire in the local grocer's shop going through a slab of cheese. The men on the forecastle were diving for whatever cover they could find, and I became aware that our lads were seeking suitable cover for themselves. I was just about to move myself when it happened.

The tow-rope had reached a straight line between our towing hook and the bitts on the bows of the *Empire Seaman*; suddenly, it was flying back towards us. It was fortunate that we surged forward with the sudden release, and that the weight of the rope caused it to fall short of *Enigma*. As it was, we rolled from side to side, causing a few broken dishes in the galley. We could now look forward to a fortnight's wait before the next suitable spring would have a chance of re-floating the *Empire Seaman*.

Our task now was to stand by the *Empire Seaman,* so that in the event of bad weather we would be at hand to give assistance. However there also was another, and perhaps more serious, reason; even at this late stage of the war, E-boats were still operating on the East Coast, and the *Empire Seaman* would be a sitting duck should one decide to come that way.

The fortnight did not pass completely uneventfuly; we held a few darts tournaments with the crew of the *Empire Seaman*, with the Collier taking turns to be hosts. we even had a game of cricket on the sands at low tide, though the time allowed for play was somewhat limited as the pitch only remained dry for about an hour, then the rollers came on uninvited.

During the second week of our standby duty, we found that we were rather low on cigarettes, and a request was made for some supplies to be sent out.

The following day a Sun Tug brought out some tins of navy 'tickler'; there were enough tins for every member of the crew and some over for our friends on the collier. It was then we found the snag: not one packet of cigarette papers was to be found on board. further more, none had been sent out. As you can imagine, there was quite a few experiments made before we settled for navy issue toilet paper gummed with condensed milk. As a cool smoke, I would not recommend it to anyone, but you could make a cigarette that would last the whole of a 'stand easy'.

A couple of days before our vigil ended we received a call to go to the assistance of the SS *Sam Nethy*, a liberty ship that had run aground on the Margate Sands during early morning fog. She was only a mile or two away from our position, and we had her refloated within the hour. It was one of the easiest jobs we ever had to undertake, a real copybook job that went like clockwork.

The great day eventually arrived when we were at last able to make our next attempt at refloating the *Empire Seaman*. The tide was good, the weather was right and the way that collier came off the hard sand was as though it had suddenly woken up from an afternoon's nap and was wondering what all the fuss was about.

We were soon heading back for Harwich; that little bar at the back of The Three Cups was like a magnet, and we had developed a strong thirst for a nice pint of cool beer.

The day after our arrival back at Harwich, we were required to go to Parkestone Quay for storing ship. The tide had just about reached the high water mark as we made our way upstream on the outside of the destroyer and frigate Trots abreast of the Quay. The skipper decided to come round, and head down stream around the topmast trot; he gave the helmsman the order to put the wheel over, and we came round head down stream between the quay and the trot-buoys. There was a vacant berth just between a couple of small patrol-type trawlers, and we headed for it. I heard the telephone ring down to stop engines, and then for slow astern as we neared the berth.

*Enigma* began to slow, but then her head began to swing to starboard towards the trawler *Fire Fly*, which was quietly lying alongside the quay at peace with the whole world. I heard the telegraph sound once more, and fully expected *Enigma* to increase stern power, but to my surprise we began to move ahead at an alarming rate. I looked as the skipper gave the telegraph a double ring astern, which would give us full emergency stern power, but the action was just too late: we had already caught the *Fire Fly* a blow amidships.

The impact sent the poor little trawler hard against the quay with a resounding thump. *Enigma* began to climb up over her midship bulwarks as our stern, which was cut away at the foot like an ice-breaker's bows, slowly rode over her side. The *Fire Fly* heeled toward us, and there was the sound of pots, pans and crockery falling from below her decks. Three heads appeared together in the hatchway leading below decks as the crew fought their way up onto the deck. Then slowly we gathered stern way, and as the weight came off the poor little *Fire Fly* rolled from side to side with further sound of breaking crockery echoing up from her messdecks below.

With red faces we crawled into our berth, and the skipper hurriedly lept on board the *Fire Fly* in an attempt to placate her now furious skipper. About a month after this incident, our skipper surprised us with the news that he was leaving the ship on medical grounds, and that a new CO would be joining in a few days time.

On a Saturday early in March our new skipper arrived. It was just on lunchtime when a slim, dark haired man of about thirty-eight years, wearing the uniform of a Lieutenant Commander came on board. This was our new CO, Lt-Com. Harry Tarbotton, RNR, MBE, a man whom we were later to learn held an extra master ticket, and had previously been a skipper for United Towing Company. Prior to joining *Enigma* he had been CO of the rescue tug *Frisky*, working out of St. John's, Newfoundland, where he had been stationed for the past two years. It was said that he had more salvage awards to his credit than any other CO in the rescue tug service.

He proved to be a man who could relax and enjoy himself, and made many friends on board. Some of the crew members he already knew, having worked with them for 'United'; he soon became affectionately known as 'Tarry' by one and all.

Soon after 'Tarry' joined us, we made a permanent berth alongside the Trinity House pier at Harwich, and shared the moorings with *Patricia*, the flag ship of Trinity House, and the old GPO ship *Monarch*. We became very friendly with the crews of these vessels, often entertaining and being entertained aboard them, so it was something of a shock when we were called out to go to the assistance of the *Monarch* when she struck a mine off the Norfolk coast some weeks later. Unfortunately, she had sunk before we could get anywhere near her; she went down with the loss of two lives, the remainder being saved by escort vessels in the vicinity.

The first big job that came our way after 'Tarry' arrived came shortly after the mate, Sid Hewitt, had left for a weekend leave in Hull. We received a signal to go to the assistance of SS *Conakrian*, a United Africa 'Palm Line' vessel. It appeared that she had 'sat' on a mine shortly after leaving Ostend laden with, of all things, V1 and V2 rockets that were being brought back to this country for examination by explosive experts. She was slowly making her way across the North Sea in a sinking condition after striking a mine.

We eventually met up with her in the Margate Roads, where she had just previously dropped anchor. She was a sorry sight; her No. 4 hold, where the main blast had been, was completely flooded and water had gradually gained a hold in the engine room, so that it had to be abandoned. Her freeboard aft was just 18 inches.

After a preliminary examination of her bulkheads it was decided to tow her around to the Warp, the anchorage to the east of Southend. It was necessary to unshackle a link in her anchor cable and buoy it, as she had no power at the winches to haul in her anchor cable.

The tow was connected during the late afternoon, and the idea was to anchor in the Warp until daylight and then to proceed to the Explosives buoy at Holehaven; all went well until just after midnight. 'Tarry' and I were keeping continuous watch, only relieving each other for meals. We were making our way across into the Barrow Deep, prior to swinging round into the Warp, when suddenly an Aldis Lamp began to flash from the bridge of *Conakrian*.

The message was short and to the point. 'Beach immediately, settling fast'. 'Tarry' went over to the chart table and pointing to the East Cant, a gradual shelving sandy shore on the Kent Coast, he said 'it's the only place'. We did not even have to alter course; it was just a matter of increasing the engine revs and keeping our fingers crossed.

What we had not bargained for was other shipping; it was a black night and we carried dimmed navigation and towing lights. The *Conakrian* was using emergency paraffin lamps; her side lights and two red 'not under command' lights at her mast head were hardly visible. We had just reached, and were beginning to cross, the main fairway below the Yantlet channel when we espied the lights and the dim outline of an escort vessel with a convoy astern just leaving the river. We gave a couple of blasts to let him know that we were heading across his course, and then a long blast and two shorts to let him know we were towing.

The escort vessel, which proved to be a destroyer, swung to pass astern of *Enigma* but did not seem to realise how far astern the *Conakrian* was. He had almost reached our tow line when it must have dawned on him, and he stopped. 'Tarry' put our telegraph at stop, then through a loud-hailer he shouted across to the destroyer to go ahead, our tow-rope having sunk sufficiently below the surface for him to do so; he hesitated for a few moments, then seeing the *Conakrian* bearing down on him, scuttled across.

We immediately took up the slack, and put on all speed to get *Conakrian* beached; the remainder of the convoy swung around the stern of *Conakrian* and headed for more sea-room. What they, and ourselves, had not noticed was an inward bound convoy just a few cable lengths the other side. We heard quite a few sound signals as the outward bound ships were caught on the wrong side of the fairway, and in one instance the sound of metal grinding against metal. I was fully expecting to see a few additional wrecks when daylight came, but all was peaceful and calm without a sign that anything had happened during the night.

With *Conakrian* beached, we were able to drop back alongside her and get our salvage pumps to work. Ron Knight, the chief engineer, donned a shallow diving outfit and descended into her engine room. After checking round, he found the reason for the engine room flooding: an inlet water valve to *Conakrian*'s main engine was still open, and the water was flowing through a fractured pipe into the engine room itself.

Coming back onto the deck, he asked one of *Conakrian*'s engine room staff, who happened to be one of our coloured brothers, for a 5/8 inch spanner. This worthy lad grinned, and said: 'Boss, I ain't got no 5/8 inch spanner, but I sure has got my bags packed'.

Eventually Ron managed to stem the flow, and we were able to pump the engine room dry. The bulk-head to No. 4 hold was shored up and on the flood tide, with the assistance of a couple of Sun tugs, we towed *Conakrian* to Holehaven buoy for discharge of her unusual cargo.

We did have a few more small jobs whilst we were based at Harwich. VE Day came, and was duly celebrated. I had previously managed to get a weekend leave, during which time I had proposed to, and had been accepted by the lady who was to become my wife.

The wedding was set for 2 June, and by some strange coincidence that was just three days after we entered the dry-dock at Immingham for a complete refit.

A Bachelor's night was held in the wardroom the evening before going on leave, and what a night that was! I had fortunately invited a sergeant and constable of the transport police to come aboard for a drink when they closed the dockyard gate just after midnight.

At 5.00 a.m. the next morning those two worthy gentlemen were assisting me and my best man 'Mac' McConnell onto the early morning tram from Grimsby with, I am pleased to say, a reasonable supply from the bond. It kept my reception party happy for a good few hours.

As I thought I had a fortnight to celebrate my nuptials, a telegram some ten days later recalling me to the ship came as something of a surprise, but not half as much as the surprise that was in store for me on rejoining *Enigma*, but more of that at later.

# CHAPTER TEN

# THE LONG HAUL

On my arrival back at Immingham from my somewhat curtailed honeymoon, I had to look twice before I eventually found my ship. It was getting towards dusk and the light was going fast. I looked toward the dry dock where I had last seen the familiar lines of *Enigma*, but she was not to be seen. Casting my eye round the dock, I espied lying on the far side of the dock a smart-looking vessel gleaming in a new coat of light grey paint.

White awnings were spread over her foredeck, and over the after end of her boat deck; from beneath the latter projected the barrel of a twelve pounder. Over each wing of the bridge, and over the flying bridge, were stretched further lengths of white canvas. If this was indeed *Enigma* she had certainly had a face lift. Her signal letters had not yet been painted in on her bows, but as she was the only vessel of her class in the dock, I had no hesitation in walking around the dock toward her.

As I walked nearer, I could see that I had not been mistaken; there is something about a vessel that will pick her out even from vessels of her own class. It could be the Turks-head on the canvas whippings of the handrails leading to the bridge, or the slight dent in the spud locker: so many familiar things which a dozen coats of paint will not hide. There could only be one answer: *Enigma* was destined for warmer regions, and me with the ink hardly dry on my marriage certificate.

As I climbed over the gangway I was met by the boson, Olley Wright. 'Hullo Second, you look as though you have lost some weight, been working hard or something?' he said. Before I had time to think up an appropriate answer, he continued with 'How do you like our new decorations, any idea where we are going?'

'Sorry bos'n,' I replied, 'Your guess would be as good as mine, though I daresay we shall learn soon enough'. I found that I was the only deck officer on board that evening; the skipper was sleeping at his home in Hull, and the mate had been drafted to another tug. I decided to get a letter off to my wife just in case our sailing orders arrived early, but on going to my cabin I found it was still in the hands of the painters; however the steward soon fixed me up in the vacant mate's cabin.

I was sitting down to breakfast with Nobby Clark, the third engineer and Bob Hannah, the chief sparks, the following morning, when the skipper arrived on board. The first thing he was to say was, 'Sorry to have interrupted your married life so early. Sid Hewitt got a draft to another tug as skipper, and our new mate will not be joining us for another two weeks.' He added, 'Get a telegram off to the missus; I have arranged lodgings for you and your wife to stay at my parents' place in Hull. You and I can work day and day about by the ship; the Bos'n is quite happy to look after things at night.'

I did not need any second bidding. By lunch time I had my wife's reply, giving her an arrival time in Grimsby the following day. I asked Tarry if he had any idea as to where we were going. He replied that as far as he knew we were to pick up a floating dock from somewhere in Scotland and tow it to Durban, and that in all we should be away for some six months at the most.

He also explained to me that I was to arrange transport into Grimsby the following day to the hydrographic office to pick up some chart folios and pilots for the trip; 'they know that you are coming and will have them ready for you', he said.

Thinking over what he had told me regarding the trip, and having found out how comfortable the mate's cabin was on the boat deck, I asked Tarry if it was possible to use the spare cabin under the starboard wing of the bridge. 'Certainly,' he replied, 'why not have words with the admiralty surveyor when he comes on board, he is due back in an hour.'

The spare cabin mentioned contained two berths, and was normally used when carrying salvage officers, or pilots. My own cabin, as I have previously mentioned, was in the port alleyway aft of the galley, and immediately over the forward boiler. This was an ideal berth in the North Atlantic or North Sea, but in the tropics where we were headed, it would be like a sauna bath. Suffice it to say that one hour later, and a bottle of gin lighter, the necessary arrangements were in hand, and in three days I was the proud possesser of a boat deck cabin with single berth, and all 'mod-cons.' I felt as though I had joined the first class passengers.

I collected the folios the next day, and was somewhat surprised when I checked them; six in all, covering our trip down to Gibraltar, the Mediterranean Sea, the Red Sea, Arabian Sea, Indian Ocean, and Mallacca Straits to Singapore. I thought at first that I had the wrong charts, but was quickly assured that they were for *Enigma*. You may have one or two slight corrections, I was told. I think that I spent the best of a fortnight in bringing them up to date.

However, I certainly enjoyed having my wife with me during those two weeks that remained in Immingham, and I shall never forget the kindness shown to us by the skipper, his wife and parents. My appreciation of Yorkshire Pudding has never flagged since those days I spent in Hull.

Larry Bound, our new mate, joined us two days before we sailed. I learnt that he had previously been mate acting master in the Trinity House vessels, and had suffered the misfortune of losing one of his crew whilst the latter was engaged in buoy-jumping when mooring at Blackwell Depot. I did look this up in the old missing persons book at Blackwall when I first joined the Police Thames Division; perhaps there might be some of our old friends who may recall the incident.

Our sailing orders eventually arrived: we were to proceed the next day to Fort William, going north about through the Pentland Firth, the shorter route through Caledonian Canal being too shallow for our draught of 18 feet 6 inches.

At Fort William we were to collect the AFD 22, an Admiralty Floating Dock of some 27,000 tons, manned by a crew of twenty – naval personnel under the command of a commissioned shipwright – and to commence towing her to Gibraltar, the final destination still being a secret to us.

We set sail for Fort William the next morning, and had a really good passage. I was officer of the watch when we made our passage through the Pentland Firth in the middle watch. I had read a number of yarns, and had some first hand accounts of the storms that rage

Mac (left), Larry (centre) and me, Singapore 1946.

in those waters, but on that night there were only a few ripples on the water, and it was as light as day with the effect of the Northern Lights.

We had neared the entrance to the Sound of Mull by eight in the morning; as I was leaving my cabin to go below for breakfast, I realised that we were in a thick bank of fog that had suddenly formed. *Enigma* was already committed within the entrance of the loch; the anchor could not be dropped as there was no bottom, the sea at that point being sixty-five to seventy fathoms deep. In those days radar was a luxury that we did not possess; all we could do was to steam at dead slow ahead on dead reckoning, keep our eyes skinned and hope that we did not get too close to the walls of rock that rose like cliffs from the loch's surface.

We did send some of the lads into the bows to shout as loud as they could and then listen for any echoes; then, as suddenly as it had formed the fog lifted, leaving us in bright sunshine to steam the remaining few miles into Loch Linnhe and on to Fort William, where we dropped anchor.

The floating dock was preparing for sea when we arrived; the travelling cranes on her high walls were being welded into a position where they could be prevented from moving in the event of bad weather, all movable gear was being stored or lashed securely to ring bolts set into her decks.

Two more days were spent in storing ship and dock; fresh water and bunkers were taken in for the first leg of what was to prove one of the longest tows by a single tug at that time, except for the compulsory assistance of a Suez Canal tug on the leg through to the Red Sea.

We left Fort William in the middle of July, making our way down past Oban, out into the Irish Sea, down the east coast of Northern Ireland, crossing over into the mouth of the St George's Channel and finally leaving Wolf Rock Lighthouse disappearing beneath the horizon as we steamed on a course that would take us one hundred miles to the westward of Cape Finistere, before turning south for the run down to Gibraltar.

On or about 8 August we had reached this position. We had averaged some five and a half knots, and were beginning to congratulate ourselves on crossing the Bay of Biscay in fine weather, but this was not to last. The wind began to freshen and veer from westerly to a northerly direction, finally settling in the north east and gusting up to force nine and ten on the Beaufort scale.

The AFD slewed away on our starboard beam, and at times appeared to be trying to reverse our respective roles. The steering became more difficult as the sea began to rise; a constant check was kept on the towrope where it passed over the strongbacks above the engine room casing, and also over the stern of the tug. Over these points, the rope was protected with wrappings of split hide and chaffing boards, which had to be constantly greased to prevent the eighteen inch manila rope from wearing at these vulnerable points.

Within an hour, the seas running up from astern had reached heights of between twenty-five to thirty feet and were rising even higher, so the skipper decided to try bringing *Enigma* round into the weather. She managed to get round to the position where she was lying with her beam into the weather, but was hampered by the tow which drastically reduced her steerage and the strong winds on her bow section; *Enigma* would not budge. She rolled almost onto her beam ends, and try as she might to get round, every sea seemed to knock her back just when she seemed to be gaining ground. It was soon decided to go back onto the original course, this being the lesser of two evils.

Shortly after this incident, the 'Gog-rope' that held the 18 inch tow rope over the stern parted. The effect on the *Enigma* was almost disasterous; as the weight of the tow came directly onto the towing hook amidships we rolled to starboard so much that the rails on the boat deck were awash, and there she stayed as every sea threatened her capsizing.

I was in the wheel-house when this incident occurred, and found myself clinging to the telegraph while my feet slid from under me. I thought at first the skipper would have given the order to knock out, this being the term to slip the towing hook. 'Hold on', he ordered the bos'n who, by this time, was standing by the hook. 'Turn thirty degrees to port', he ordered the helmsman, 'and hold it there'.

The next ten minutes that it took to re-secure the Gog-rope and pull the tow rope back over the stern seemed like an eternity. *Enigma* rolled in a sickening movement, and the hands on the deck worked miracles as every movement she made seemed designed to throw them into the scuppers; she resented being hog-tied. How no one was seriously injured was little short of a miracle, and it was with relief once more that we turned on to our course running before the wind.

As might be expected, we lost our dinner that day on the floor of the galley; those of us that could still stomach food were offered corned beef or cheese sandwiches.

It was decidedly not our day when, just thirty minutes after replacing the Gog-rope, our towing hawser parted on the stern rail. There was nothing we could do about reconnecting the tow; our spare tow rope was stored in the after holder, and to open this, as would be necessary when streaming the rope, would be little short of suicide.

A message was passed to the dock asking if all was well with them, and on being informed they were okay, we informed them of our intention to stand by for the weather to improve before trying to reconnect the tow.

The Skipper decided to turn and run back into the weather for a few miles to a position where he could keep an eye on the dock, ready to move in should it prove necessary. We kicked around under half speed ahead; *Enigma* responded well now that she was unhampered.

sliding down the far side of a roller, she rushed head on towards a wave that towered threateningly above her, then just as it looked as if she would bury herself, her bows began to climb higher and higher as she rode the wave; not a drop of water came over the bow. It was like riding a roller coaster at a fairground: *Enigma* proved herself to be a wonderful sea-boat when running into those giant seas. On reaching our selected point, we swung round stern on to the wind, and stopped our engines.

The effect was amazing. We were sailing along at a fair speed, the built up bridge and funnel were acting like a sail, and we began to overhaul and eventually passed the floating dock. Thus every two hours it was necessary to repeat the manoeuvre, choosing the right moment for the turn. This was to be the way of life for the next three days. I decided to sleep on the floor of my cabin after being deposited there on two occasions during these turns. I wonder if perhaps I had given cause for discomfort.

We were rather surprised, on taking a sight the following day, to find that we were averaging three and a half knots, giving us eighty-five miles for a day's run, and this was practically on our course.

Taking the number of times that we turned back into the wind, our true speed sailing before the wind was something like five knots. The weather eventually moderated sufficiently for us to renew the tow rope, and we continued on our way to Gibraltar.

We had been joined by a soldier-class armed trawler, the *Grenadier,* as escort and fortunately she carried radar, for when we were just a day out of Gibraltar we came into thick fog. *Grenadier* was able to keep us informed of other shipping movements about it, and as we steamed ahead we sounded our towing signal, one long blast and two short. We were suddenly surprised to hear the ringing of a ship's bell.

At first we looked at each other in amazement. Here we were in five hundred fathoms and someone was trying to tell us that he was lying at anchor; it just did not make sense. Our escort could not help us, he was as puzzled as ourselves, and could make nothing out on his radar screen that would fit the bell.

We eventually learned from the young RNVR Sub-Lieutenant on the floating dock that his CO had decided to ring it when he heard us blowing to make sure people would know he was about.

Our stay in Gibraltar lasted for four days, during which time stores, water and fuel were taken aboard for the next leg. Among the stores we had managed to acquire were two five and a half inch carpenters stoppers. These were of a heavy steel construction, fashioned like a book. The two metal leaves, hinged on one side, would open to accommodate the wire and a steel wedge in a grooved channel. When closed, it gripped the wire firmly; two stout chains were led from one end for fixing to a ring bolt in the deck. We utilised these stoppers by adding a wire hawser to our end of the tow rope and allowing the tow rope to be just clear of the tug's stern.

The wire was then led through one stopper, and made fast to the after deck, thus acting as the gog-rope; the other was used directly from the towing hook. In this way the rope was never subject to further chaffing, and when the wire showed any sign of wear it was a simple matter to slip two or three inches at the hook, and then at the after stopper without losing any way on the towing vessel. We never needed another rope to be replaced on *Enigma* during my next twelve months aboard her. This was a considerable saving when weighing the cost of a new rope; even in those days they cost around one thousand pounds.

We left Gibraltar bound for Port Said for passage through the Suez Canal; the weather was fine and we were soaking up the sunshine. On the second day out from Gibraltar, we ran into a beam swell that was to stay with us for most of the way. *Enigma* rolled continuously in long slow movements.

A rather funny incident occured just after I had been relieved on the afternoon watch. My job as second mate also entailed, besides navigating, being the gunnery officer, victualling stores officer, and lastly, as we carried no sick berth attendant, the officer in charge of the sick bay. Unpaid of course, unwanted and perhaps unqualified should be added. In any case, our weekly paper, *The Enigmatic Times*, carried a number of adverts referring to the treatment supped at Gaster's Gruesome Grotto, and the sovereign remedy for all ills, Castor Oil. I explained that I was only following the instructions found in the Ship's Masters Medical Guide; it must have worked well, as my clients did not make too many calls on my service.

On the day in question, one of the two signalmen who shared a cabin on the port side of the boat deck with six seamen gunners came to me to tell me that seaman gunner Westwood, a tall fairheaded lad, had cut his head pretty badly and was in need of treatment. I told him to bring the injured person along to the sick bay where I would be getting ready to receive him. The door of the sick bay was open; whilst I was preparing antiseptic and dressings, I heard a noise in the alleyway outside the door, and on looking up espied my patient supported on either side by two of his colleagues. I must confess that I did a double take – his head looked one gory mess.

I hurriedly assisted him onto the couch to prepare him for treatment, and was on the point of sending for the skipper for a second opinion, when I noticed some of the gore that had transferred itself to my hands and felt strangely sticky. I transferred a little to my lips, there could be no mistake, and it was pussers issue strawberry jam. I was on the point of tearing a strip off them when I noticed that the patient was almost out on his feet, and on washing a few square inches of jam from his head, found a gash some two inches long.

On asking what had happened, I was informed that just after leaving Gibraltar where we had been on VJ Day, permission had been granted to undarken ship. One of the ports in the gunners mess had been permanently blacked out by reason of a bunk stanchion being immediately in front of the deadlight so that it could not be raised. The lads had got round this by removing the hinge pin and placing the deadlight on top of one of their lockers; whilst they were sitting down to tea the deadlight had slid off the locker as the ship rolled, and had struck the unfortunate gunner on the back of his head causing him to slump forward into the plate of jam that was on the mess table.

A few days after this incident, I was called to look at the third engineer Nobby Clark; he had developed a severe pain in his side and was running a temperature. I confirmed my theory by checking the medical guide: Nobby was suffering from acute appendicitis. A vessel was sent out to meet us from Malta, then about one hundred miles away, and I had the job of transferring him in the ship's motor boat. This was no easy matter in the beam swell that was running, as every time *Enigma* rolled, the sides of the boat were threatened by the rubbing band that projected from her side at right angles, and were almost a foot thick. I was more than relieved when we had hooked on, and had been lifted clear of the water on our return.

We eventually arrived at Port Said, where we spent a further four days before continuing our journey through the canal. The passage through the canal was very interesting; a Suez Canal tug took over the tow, leaving us to act as 'Tail End Charlie' on the stern of the dock. In this position we acted as a brake whenever a ship passed us on the way from the Red Sea. When this happened we would ease over to the port side of the canal until the ship had passed, and then continue on our way.

We spent that evening in the bitter Lakes at Ismalia. Here we encouraged some of our non-swimmers to have a go, and two of them swam for the first time in the buoyant waters of the lake, after that there was no holding them back. I nearly broke my neck when diving in from the boat deck; I soon learned to keep my head between my arms when in those waters.

The heat below decks during the day was unbearable, and where the sun had been baking the metal work during the day it was possible to get a nasty burn on any unprotected skin on the arms and legs.

We continued our journey through to the Red Sea the next day; the heat was unbearable and a number of the stokehold staff went down with heat exhaustion, and had to be brought up on deck and wrapped in wet blankets to bring their body temperature down quickly.

A frigate that was acting as our escort moved around us in circles to provide enough draught for his ventilation. Meanwhile, we steamed

Aboard a DUKW checking islands in Straits for POW graves 1946. Jack second from right.

along at our steady five-and-a-half knots, hardly raising enough draught to blow the smoke away from our funnel. Nearly half the engine room staff required medical attention on arrival at Aden; most of us were suffering from prickly heat, and had sweated off a number of pounds. Salt tablets were the order of the day, together with mepacrine which made us look like oriental gentlemen.

One afternoon, whilst we were lying alongside an American-built Lease-Lend tug, *Oriana*, a native who was a member of a working party on board her fell over the side. He was quickly rescued, but needed resuscitation; without thinking, his rescuers laid him on his front on the patterned steel deck and commenced working on him. He quickly began to recover and struggled to get up; it was only then that they realised that a neat pattern of diamonds was branded into the exposed skin of his chest and stomach.

The next and last leg of our tow was the longest, taking nearly five weeks for the crossing of the Indian Ocean to Ceylon and Trincomalee. We were little more than a week out of Aden when our refrigerator went on the blink. I must say that the cook rose to the occasion: what he didn't manage to do with rice and corned beef is not in any cookery book. We had it boiled, baked, fried, made into fritters, curried, and I think on one occasion in a stew with the corned beef. It got so that the mere mention of rice would make us shudder. 'Please God, let there be spuds in Trinco' was the heartfelt prayer of everyone on board.

We arrived there in the second week of October; our journey had taken three months, steaming some seven thousand two hundred odd miles. To say that we were pleased to give up our burden was something of an understatement; the sheer joy to look aft and not to have to look at the all too familiar lines of the floating dock was a relief.

Our mail had finally caught up with us, the first since leaving Immingham, and there were bumper bundles for all, but best of all we had some fresh meat and vegetables. What the meat was I do not know, but it went down like chicken, and many a satisfied face got up from the table.

We were to spend a week in Trincomalee before sailing to our next destination; not for us the quick return to home waters promised before we left the UK. We were bound for the Far East. What we were to encounter is another story yet to come.

# CHAPTER ELEVEN

# ENIGMA IN THE SOUTH SEAS

On leaving Trincomalee we set course for Akyab, a little inlet on the Burma Coast to the north east across the Bay of Bengal. Akyab was an important place during the advance of the Fourteenth Army down the Malay Peninsular against the Imperial Japanese Armies.

Two days out from Trinco, we ran into a rainstorm the like of which I doubt I shall ever see again. For a whole day we ploughed our way through it, blind to anything beyond the bows. It was raining solidly, and the sky was darkened as though the sun had been eclipsed. At intervals of a half minute or so, the whole scene would be lit with a ghostly light, as lightening flashed from cloud to sea, followed almost instantaneously by tremendous claps of thunder that echoed and re-echoed across the skies. My faith in our lightning conductors was not very strong, and I looked very apprehensively at the tops of our masts that seemed to be scraping the bottoms of the dark clouds as they hung low over our heads.

We reached Akyab after a run lasting approximately seven days; for most of that time the sky had been overcast, and we had to rely on wireless bearings and dead reckoning for our navigation. Our stay was only a matter of twenty-four hours, but it was long enough for us to accept a challenge from the local port operating group of the Royal Engineers to play a game of football. I must say that after our prolonged time afloat, most of us were in need of a bit of exercise and we were well and truly trounced by the challengers.

The following day we left Akyab behind as we steamed towards Singapore towing a large steel raft, commonly known as a 'Rhino Ferry' and used to assist landings of Army tanks, guns, and heavy equipment in shallow waters. It measured some one hundred feet in length by some thirty feet in the beam, but was very easy to tow at a good ten knots.

Our trip down to the Malacca Straits was fairly uneventful; the weather had improved a great deal, and there was a danger of receiving severe burns from the sun if exposed for too long a period. this was soon discovered by some of the lads who had taken to sleeping on deck during their off watch periods.

On the first morning after our having entered the Straits, I was being relieved by the mate and was standing talking to him on the starboard wing of the bridge, when Nobby Clark, our third engineer, came up to join us for a chat before turning in, it being just 4.00 a.m. and still fairly dark.

I had my back to the forward rail of the bridge and was facing Nobby; suddenly he stuttered, 'MINE, look at the size of the f*****g thing!' We swivelled round, and there, just a matter of about twenty yards away and almost under our starboard bow, was the biggest mine I had ever, or would ever, wish to see. Larry Bound, the mate, immediately ordered the helmsman to steer port ten degrees, followed almost at once by steady, come ten degrees starboard. We practically waltzed around that mine, and ran to the rail to watch it disappear astern, passing our side at almost spitting distance.

Our next worry was for our tow, which luckily was unattended; it must have been a close thing, for we could still see the dark outline following in our wake well past the time it would have taken the mine to reach it. A message was despatched to the senior officer operations in Singapore regarding the mine, so that a message could be sent to the shipping operating in the area. I was most thankful when I left the bridge to see Larry peering ahead through a pair of night glasses. I think it helped me to sleep a lot sounder.

Singapore was reached the next day, and after depositing our tow we made for the Keppel Dockyard, where we were to berth for a few days whilst restoring ship and bunkering ready for our next task. We were soon informed what it was to be when the senior officer rescue tugs put in an appearance that afternoon. We were to proceed

Singapore 1946, swimming party going ashore, Jack steering, at centre.

to Manus, a small island in the Admiralty Islands in the Bismark Archipelago, off the coast of New Guinea.

I had to call at the hydrographic office to pick up the necessary charts for the trip. The chap in charge was most apologetic with regard to the condition of the folios. Some of them had not been corrected since the day the Japs had entered Singapore, and a number of them were missing altogether. I found that he had not understated matters. I was kept busy for some considerable time trying to get them up to date with the information available at the time. In one section where a chart was missing from the folio, we would have to steam for some one hundred and twenty miles through coral seas and atolls, where coral build ups could change in a matter of weeks.

We set sail via the Straits of Sumatra, the Java Sea and the Celebes, crossing and re-crossing the equator three times. Whilst on passage through the Java Sea, we ran in to a vast area that was infested by sea snakes. There must have been thousands of them; they were about eight to ten feet in length, with green and yellow markings. We decided to have a bit of practice with the rifles, and soon found that when hit they would leap up out of the water to a height of some ten or twelve feet before falling back into the sea. I was told on good authority that they were deadly poisonous, so we had little qualms regarding their slaughter. We had fair weather all the way on this trip, though when we needed good visibility for our trip across the unchartered section we encountered sea mists, and had to keep our eyes peeled for the unexpected.

When we were within sight of Manus we tried to raise them over the radio for harbour directions. Our only chart of the harbour was on a large-scale chart. The harbour itself was depicted just big enough for one sounding to be shown, and this was twenty-seven fathoms. We must have been in a radio black spot because we did not get a reply, and so had to steam in under our own guess-work.

On reaching the centre of the harbour the skipper decided to anchor, and gave the necessary order. The anchor rattled out in a cloud of red dust particles, the bell rang for one cable, then for two, three, four and still no bottom. 'Hold it' said the skipper. At that moment a Yankee-trooper that was propping up a quay invited us to tie up alongside him. We did not need any second bidding and made fast alongside the MTS *Antigua*, and were made very welcome. I went on board and asked if I could take a look at his charts, and found that there was a deep hole some twenty feet in diameter and one hundred fathoms deep in the centre of the harbour. We had found it in one go!

We had timed our arrival in Manus to the week before Christmas 1945. Our refrigerator was once more defective, so it was wonderful to be asked to share our Christmas and New Year with our American hosts. They on their part were glad to have us, as they were what are called 'Dry Ships'. We provided the Christmas spirits, and they supplied as much food as we could tuck away. In fact, the meal I put away in the wardroom of the *Antigua* on Christmas Day would not have disgraced the table of the Savoy.

I was able to restock our chart folios from the Australian naval base on the island, so that we could plot our course back to Singapore fairly safely.

A few days after the New Year, the *Antigua* took her leave. We were sorry to see her go as we had made good friends on board. We went to an anchorage off a small island in the bay where there were facilities for swimming inside a safety net that had been rigged by the American Forces.

Jack Gaster, Sub-Lieutenant, Singapore, 1946.

Whilst lying there we were using our Pulling boat, as the motor launch had engine trouble. On returning to the ship one afternoon from our daily swim, I was in the shower removing the salt that had dried on my skin. Suddenly I heard the mate calling for me to join him on the after deck, and he sounded as though he was in a hurry. I went out as I was, in my birthday suit. On reaching the after deck

I could see the cause of his excitement. Two of the engine room staff had gone off in the pulling boat in an attempt to recover a small American landing craft that had drifted past towards the harbour entrance. It was unattended and although they had managed to get a line on it, they were gradually losing ground and were drifting further away on a one knot current that ran through the harbour.

'Come on in,' called Larry, and dived over the side making for the boat; I followed, though I must confess I had not the speed of my senior. I should say I did not think I had the speed, because I had a sudden chill fear strike me. That morning, when I was up on the bridge, I had seen a hammer-head-shark go swimming through the harbour at a leisurely pace.

It suddenly it occurred to me that even now he could be studying my naked body with mouth-watering interest. I really started to swim then; in fact, it would not have surprised me to learn I had been planing. I passed Larry as though he was treading water, and on reaching the boat I was onboard before I knew I got there. Larry came alongside and asked what all the panic was about. I hardly got the words out of my mouth when he was alongside me. With the four of us pulling we soon got back alongside *Enigma*, and the landing craft was collected from us.

A couple of mornings after this incident, one of our engine room staff had woken up to relieve the chap who was supposed to be on duty below. Fortunately he was a chap who did not have to be called; after many years of watch keeping he could wake up on the dot. This morning he made his way down into the engine room expecting to see the duty fireman, a young Newfoundlander named Parsons, but he was not to be found. Our friend checked his bunk to see if he had already turned in, but it was empty. He then returned aft, and was on the point of calling all hands when he heard a faint cry for help. The sound seemed to be coming from over the stern, and on investigating further, young Newfy, as we called him, was found sitting on the rudder head that was just above the water level under the stern counter. It appeared that the young stoker had come on to the deck for a breath of fresh air, and had sat on the rail with his back to the water. He must have fallen asleep, or as one unkindly soul put it, 'He must have dropped off'. Anyway, it appears he had been sitting on the rudder head for nearly an hour, and was more than pleased to hear someone on deck.

At last we were ready to sail. We were to tow the Admiralty Floating Dock No. 20 from Manus back to Singapore. The AFD 20 was of the same size as the 22 that we had towed to Trinco from Scotland, and our speed was exactly the same, five and a half knots at a steady plod. All went well for the first seven days, and then the personnel on the floating dock informed us that they were making water forward. It appeared that a number of rivets had sprung, and that we should have to put in somewhere in order that they could get to work on them.

The place we chose was a natural harbour with an inner lagoon; I believe I have the correct spelling when I say that it was Manaquari. sufficient to say it was the north coast of what was then Dutch New Guinea. The local population consisted of three Dutch Army officers, seven hundred native troops, and seven thousand, give or take a few, Japanese prisoners of war.

Whilst waiting for the repairs to the floating dock to be carried out, we took advantage of the chance to do a little exploring. My one and only attempt to gather coconuts from the top of the palms resulted in my being attacked by a red ant colony that disputed my right to be up that particular tree. I was made to beat a very hasty retreat to the safety of the lagoon before I could get rid of them.

The day before we left Manaquari, we were having a last swim in the lagoon; most of us were wearing canvas shoes to protect ourselves from the sharp coral. Just as we were leaving the water, I heard the chief engineer scream out, 'My feet, my feet'. At first I thought that he had been attacked by a small shark, though we had been assured that none had entered the lagoon for many years. We rushed to his aid and carried him ashore: his feet looked as though they had been used as a pin cushion. He had unfortunately trod on a sea urchin, with the result it had shed its poisonous barbs into his feet. An old native woman who looked as though she badly needed an uplift folded her arms across her chest and said in 'pigeon' English, 'him by and by mort'.

The only doctor on the base at that time was Japanese, and he could only offer something that looked like a yellow paste to put on the chief's feet, but it did nothing to ease his agony. We got back on board and radioed for assistance. The call was answered by a frigate, HMS *Crane*, who was coming to act as escort vessel and was only a very short distance away. The MO from *Crane* came aboard and brought a supply of kaolin and pain killing tablets. I was instructed to apply as hot as possible to the patient's feet every two hours, in order to keep the poison down in his lower limbs. This I did until we reached Morotai four days later, when a launch was sent out to take him to the base hospital, and it was not a day too soon. I am pleased to say a good recovery was made after three weeks' treatment.

After dropping Ronnie Knight, the chief engineer, at Morotai, we set course for Macasser, but were soon having trouble from our tail end shaft that was beginning to run very hot. Another tug that was in the area, the *Griper,* joined us a day out of Macasser and relieved us of our tow. We then went ahead with the intention of putting in to Macasser to take on water for the *Griper* and the *Crane*, so that they would not have to stop. On our way in to Macasser in the early hours of the morning, we were shaping to use the main entrance as shown on our chart. I had in fact just been relieved by the mate, and also the skipper, due to the fact we were about to enter harbour, when I heard the telegraph ring down and the engine drop to slow revs.

Shortly after this I heard the telegraph again; this time the engines stopped. As we were still some way out from the port, I thought this was strange and decided to have a look up top. On arriving on the bridge I could see that the skipper was worried; we appeared to be running into shallow water where none was shown on the chart. Also we had stirred up a lot of silt behind us. We barely had water under us, and at this moment an Aldis lamp started flashing to us from a small vessel just inside the harbour. 'Use the Northern entrance, in entrance mined and blocked', came the terse message. We eased ourselves gently away from the shallows, and crept into the new channel.

By midday we had taken on sufficient water for our companion ships, and left to join them outside the harbour. Then we returned to top up once more, only to find that we would have to wait until the reservoir had filled up sufficiently. It had suffered damage during the Japanese occupation and only held a much reduced amount, and it would take another day before there would be enough water fed into it from the surrounding hills.

The following morning whilst working on the flying bridge, I noticed a battle class destroyer making for the Main Entrance at a fairly fast speed, I called the bunting tosser, and got him to send the same message that we had received the day before. The message was acknowledged almost as soon as it was sent, and the destroyer looked as though she had been fitted with disc brakes; I have never seen a ship manoeuvre as easily.

Following her at some distance was a large American freighter. I asked the signal man to repeat the message to her. Time after time we tried but no answer; she still ploughed on towards the main entrance as though to disprove our warning. Suddenly across the expanse of water that divided us came the noise of a dull explosion; at first I thought that it was too far away to be the American, but she had stopped and then the Destroyer sent us a message on her lamp to go to the assistance of the SS *Sea Satyr*, longitude, etc., latitude, etc. I had to look at the chart before I realised it was the ship we had tried to contact for the last fifteen minutes. She had sat on a mine that had exploded under her number four hold. We were soon out and alongside her; there were no serious injuries and her tank tops in number four hold appeared to be holding.

Before the Captain could protest we had our tow rope on the bows and towed her into the harbour. As soon as she was safely moored we dropped alongside again and put our pumps to work whilst the bulkheads were checked and few sprung rivets were replaced. In all the whole operation had taken less than a couple of hours. The reason she had got off so lightly was the fact she had one hundred tons of rice in that hold for Macassar, and this had helped to minimise the damage to the tank tops in that hold. We found out afterwards that she was on her maiden voyage, and was delivering her cargo to the liberated populations of the East Indies.

We left Macassar the next day for Singapore at a much reduced speed. The trouble with the shaft was gradually increasing, and the hose had to be played on it continuously until we dropped anchor in the Roads at Singapore, then she just refused to go astern to straighten the cable; her shaft had seized solid. Arrangements were made, and we were towed by a harbour service tug to the Empire Dry Dock.

*Enigma* was not repaired for some three months as most of the spares had to be shipped out from the UK I stayed with her for a time,

Taking it easy in Singapore, July 1946.

and then left her on promotion to mate of the rescue tug *Assiduous,* which was also based in Singapore. There I had several interesting jobs until I made my passage home in December of 1946 for my demob, which by that time was some six months overdue.

*Enigma* was taken over by the Singapore Harbour Board, and a number of her officers stayed on. Harry Tarbotton, the skipper, had returned to the United Towing Company in Hull. The last I heard of that gentleman was from one of his fellow tug skippers, to say that he had taken an appointment as dock master of the King George V Dock in Hull.

I learned a lot from Harry Tarbotton; he was a man who never knew the meaning of the word impossible. If there was a way to salvage a ship, then he would find it. He came from a special breed of men who had manned sea-going tugs all their lives.

CHAPTER TWELVE

# ASSIDUOUS

Constant, hardworking, diligent; those are the definitions given in the Oxford Dictionary for the name of my new ship the *Assiduous*, and it was to me that I thought they should refer after my first few weeks on that vessel, for I was certainly thrown in at the deep end by my new Captain, Lt J. J. Davis RNR., who was her master.

I joined the *Assiduous* one afternoon at the beginning of June 1946, having been sent to her from the *Enigma*, which was still in the hands of the dockyard maties in the Keppel Dockyard in Singapore.

My reason for being there became apparent when I saw her; the senior officer of rescue tugs in Singapore, a Lieut Cmdr. Thompson, had sent me to her on promotion to chief officer to get her ready for the Flag Officer Malaya's inspection, which was due in some six weeks. It would appear that FOM had paid a surprise visit to the *Assiduous* whilst she was lying alongside the dockyard at Seleter one morning, to find that there was no one on the gangway, and on walking aboard half the crew were stretched out on the foredeck and the ship was in a very dirty condition. The result of all this was the number one and the chief engineer were posted to other vessels and two volunteers, 'you and you'!! (myself and Bill Watts – a Sub-Lt (E) T124T) were given the job of making her look something.

I reported to my new CO on the bridge that was somewhat smaller than that of the *Enigma*, with the chart room and the captain's cabin leading off abaft, squeezed very tightly between the bridge and the funnel. Unlike the *Enigma* there was a walkway around the front of the bridge, and I must say that the wheelhouse and chartroom were immaculate and all the brass work, of which there was plenty, gleamed like burnished gold and the floors were well polished. This I understood later, was the work of the signalman that she carried, but the rest of the ship was in stark contrast.

The Captain, or J. J. as he was called by most of the crew, though not to his face, gave me a free hand in the running of the ship; 'I don't care how you do it, or what arrangements you make in working the ship, you have my full support in getting her ready, just ask for anything that you want'. I decided to go and inspect my quarters and was quite pleased with the size and the position that it occupied amidships under the bridge, where I was handy to all the working of the ship.

However, the cabin was long due for a spring clean. I called down to the second steward who was responsible for my quarters, and got him to fetch me a bucket of hot water with a handful of soda in it and a bar of pusser's hard soap. Soogy Moogy was the term for it on board ship. I then set to, and gave the cabin paintwork and the floor a good scrub until every last bit of grime was removed.

Sporting a crew cut. With *Assiduous*, 1946.

My next job was polishing of furniture and fittings, and finally the brass port and cabin light on its gimbals. It looked a treat and felt more like home. Having stowed all my personal gear, I called down to the second steward and asked what he thought of it. 'It looks very good, I doubt if I could have done better myself.' he said. 'Then you had better have a try,' I enjoined, 'For this is how I want it kept in the future.'

I took stock of the crew list, and was not very happy with what I saw. Half the crew had been released on age and service and were on their way home; instead of a chief petty officer boatswain, a leading seaman quartermaster, six ABs and four GDs and two signalmen, I had one AB, six ODs and one signalman. To make matters worse, having met the second officer, a Sub-Lt Tom King RNVR T124T who hailed from Erith in Kent, and like myself was a freeman waterman and lighterman from the River Thames, I found that he was sailing home the next day also on age and service release.

I went and had a word with the skipper, and recommended that the crew that remained be promoted, the able seaman, a chap named Spoors, to quartermaster acting boatswain, which would give him a leading seaman rate, this being long overdue, and the ordinary seaman to be made able seaman. They all had sufficient service, and this would give them some incentive and perhaps boost the moral of the crew as a whole. The new chief engineer, a Sub-Lt (E) T124T William Watts, who also like Tom King hailed from Erith, and had previously worked as an engineer in one of the Watkins Tugs on the Thames, had similar problems.

I think that he also had to make the best use he could of a depleted staff, and made several recommendations for promoting those worthy to the ranks needed to maintain an efficient engine room staff. I called the deck hands aft at the first opportunity, and informed them of the forthcoming inspection by the Flag Officer; as you can imagine they were not entirely filled with joy at the prospect of working flat out for the next three weeks.

I also informed them that the tropical routine now being worked where hands secured in the afternoon would have to go by the board until such time that we could see the ship looking presentable. I could see that they were by now looking decidedly unhappy, so I thought that I had better put a bit of sugar on the pill and told them of their recommendations to a higher rate, but stressed that they would be on an acting rate until they proved their efficiency.

I need not have worried; from then, as one, they set to the task of restoring some of the pride back on the *Assiduous*. I found myself an old pair of khaki shorts and some sandals, picked up a wire brush and a chipping hammer and joined the lads down on the after deck and commenced scaling a section of the bulwarks that was in a pretty bad state.

The air was full of rust particles that adhered itself to our sweaty bodies as the sound of chipping hammers and wire brushes together with the scrapers filled the afternoon. There would be no peace for anyone wishing to take an afternoon nap on board the other vessels around us. We had been working steadily for an hour or so when I happened to notice one or two of the lads leave the after deck for five minutes at a time. One of these was close to where I was working; I called back, and asked 'Where's he off too?' 'To the heads'; he replied 'for a smoke?' I asked.

Preparing for Admiral inspection in Singapore 1946, (Jack Gaster top left, facing camera).

He made no reply before I said that if he wanted to smoke then carry on, but get on with the job in hand. There were very few breaks after that, except for the very welcome cup of tea to wash the dust from our throats as the afternoon wore on. Hands to secure was piped at the end of the second dog watch, and as the lads left to take a much needed shower before they had their tea, I looked around to see the results of their efforts and was well pleased. They had made a good start on what was to be a long, tiring job. I went and had a shower and a change into some clean clothing before joining the rest of the officers in the small wardroom for a pre-dinner drink.

I think that most of us were too tired to contemplate a run ashore that night. We were down to two deck and two engineer officers, which in harbour was not a problem, but left plenty for each of us to get on with. The other member of the wardroom was a radio officer, a young Welsh chap who was rather quiet and kept to his radio room for most of the time.

That first evening I was looking for something to do; I thought that I would have a wander round ship to see if anything required immediate attention. I know that I had already told the lads that the topside was of prime importance, so that the ship showed at least a semblance of being a naval vessel, and that anything below decks would have to take second place. So it came as a bit of a shock and somewhat of a pleasant surprise to see when looking into the seaman's mess, the lads busy with paint pot and brushes giving their quarters a much needed face lift, and this after a hard day's graft on the after deck.

From there I looked into the firemen's mess; again here I was taken aback by the contrast between the two messes. It was in a shocking state. It looked as though they had never bothered to clean or change the bedding since the ship had first commissioned, and I would think that the hands must have come straight up out of the engine room or boiler room and dropped straight to their bunks. I did not stay there too long, as I would have exploded; the first thing in the morning, after a chat with the skipper and chief engineer, I saw the chief steward who was also responsible for the ship's bedding and linen, and got him to indent for a complete change of bedding from the shore base as a matter of urgency.

There was very little that could be done in the way of cleaning after all that time. There were some old towing springs flaked out on the after deck that were in a very poor condition, being full of rust and with plenty of sprigs that endangered the hands when handling them. Theses were of 5½ inch to 6 inch in diameter, and approximately sixty fathoms in length. I managed to get rid of them and replaced them with some new lengths.

These were flaked out on a wooden platform some three inches above a diamond patterned deck that was also in a very rusty condition, so much so that the patterning had almost disappeared below the rust. J. J. came up with an idea that he had learned when working with a Dutch skipper some years before. We sprayed the whole of the after deck with gas oil and left it for a few hours. Then, using wire brushes the rust seemed to be easier to remove. Again, another coat of gas oil was applied, which left the deck somewhat better looking, before spraying over with seawater. This left the whole of the deck with a black, shiny non-slip finish, and the oil residue prevented the rust from reforming. This operation was repeated about once a month and the after deck, once the engine room casing and the bulwarks and ventilators together with the capstan had been painted, looked really good.

We still had some three weeks to go before the inspection was due when J. J. was called to the NOIC's office in Singapore for a briefing. It would seem that the Dutch Shell Oil Company were going to lay an oil pipe line off the Borneo Coast at Miri, and we would be required to assist in the towing of the pipe, which was to be supported by one of their own tankers, and was some four miles in length in a direct line straight off the shore.

Apparently the pipe was already completed, and was in a trench constructed by their engineers supported on trolleys that ran on rails the whole length of the trench. J. J. was a little circumspect about the one and only towrope that we had on board. It was the usual 18 inch manilla and looked in reasonable condition, but had parted just short of the eye on a previous job, and although it had been respliced and had a new hard eye and towing link, he was still doubtful about using it.

We asked the Naval Stores if they had a new tow rope at hand, but they could not help us, so we then settled for a 120 fathom 5½ inch diameter flexible steel wire rope with an eye splice at each end. This I had flaked out on the after table over the steering quadrant, having first led the outer eye to the towing hook. The remaining turns after the first thirty feet or so were seized with some inch line, so that they could be cut as required when running on ahead of the tow before the main weight came on the tow itself. This, I am pleased to say, worked quite well when the time came, and the whole operation went without a hitch, that is with the exception that J. J. and myself had to work six hour watches, splitting the afternoon to three hours a piece.

The run to Miri from Singapore, some one thousand miles, took a little under four days sailing; the weather was fine and it was a relief to be under way. I was able to get some practise in with my navigation that had almost been non existent for some six months, and was surprised that my results were favourable to those obtained by J. J., who was using an American system for working out his observations. Apart from a day waiting for the Dutch to prepare the tankers for their part of the day's task, we had very little to do except try to catch some of the sharks that swam around us in large numbers, though with little success as they appeared to break every line that was used.

Following the successful operation, we had to escort a larger type MFV back to Singapore; her maximum speed was a little under eight knots, and we had to keep easing our speed to enable her to remain on station, so it was with some relief that she agreed to be taken in tow after some six hours. The difference to our speed was hardly discernable, though we kept it at about ten knots to prevent any undue strain on her bows. Apart from running in to a line squall that threatened to tear our awnings away one afternoon, the return trip was uneventful, though possibly a little tiring.

So some ten days after leaving Seleter, we were back to resume our task of restoring the *Assiduous* to her former pride and glory. I learned from the chief that the *Assiduous* had started her career as a rescue tug, not, as I thought, under the White Ensign, but under the Red Ensign, and managed by Watkins Towing Company of Gravesend of all people. I am not sure just how long that they managed her, but as I understand it, they did not get on too well and she reverted to Admiralty control under T124T, so could this, then, be the cause of the hold that the rust had on her after such a short life?

The day came nearer for the inspection, but this was put back when J. J. got his age and service release through, and he left on passage

Painting of HMS *Assiduous*, W142.

home. My new captain was Kenneth Knight, a Lt RNR. He was newly promoted from mate of the *Bustler*, one of the larger Motor Tugs of the Growler or Turmoil Class. At first he was a little put-out by the fact that we did not have a permanent gangway watchman posted, but after some explanation of what had been achieved in the past three weeks with a much depleted crew, he reluctantly agreed to leave things as they were until after the inspection.

Again we were given another job with a sister tug, the *Griper*; she was the tug that relieved the *Enigma* of her tow when we developed engine troubles, or to be precise, tail end shaft troubles when towing the floating dock from Manus to Singapore. Our tow this time was to be the Japanese cruiser *Takao* that had been sunk in Seleter Harbour by one of our X-Craft, the miniature subs operated by our frogmen, for which action they had been awarded the Victoria Cross.

The *Takao* had been raised and patched up for her last voyage that was to end in the Indian Ocean, just to the west of the Malacca Straits, where she would be sunk in some deep water away from the normal shipping lanes. I told the skipper of the trouble that J. J. had previously experienced with the 18 inch manilla, but he thought it looked okay, and decided to use it. I had still got the flexible steel wire rope flaked out aft should it be necessary, but at that time had only seized the first fifty fathoms for a straight up and down connection of the tow.

The *Takao* was manoeuvred out of her berth by a couple of the smaller Saint class tugs, and was moving ahead at about one and a half – two knots when we positioned ourselves under her head to pass the tow. Up went the messenger rope, then the towing spring (some sixty fathom of 5½ inch wire), before the 18 inch Manilla rope started to stream over the stem rail between the two gog pins. I waited till the bowman on the Takao indicated that the tow was fast before giving the go ahead signal to the skipper. We went ahead, slowly streaming the tow rope astern of us whilst I kept an eye on the remaining turns in the hold; I held up my arms to signal stop engines whilst we waited for the strain to take up on the tow. Nothing happened; we just kept moving forward, with no sign of the rope taking any strain. It soon became evident that the rope had parted; it must have been rotted through.

I passed the information to the captain through the deck phones, and then recovered all the rope remaining at our end. The Japanese crew, of which there must have been nearly fifty on the fore deck, had no power on their capstans, and they just ditched their section of the tow. We manoeuvred under her bow once more, and I passed up the end of the towing wire.

Meanwhile the skipper was moving slowly ahead as I carefully cut each seizing in turn, watching the struggle of the deck party on the *Takao* as they tried to reach the towing bollards on the foredeck with the end of the wire rope. I tried to get the skipper to take our way off, as it looked at one time that they would not make the bollard, but with just a few more seizings to go they made it, and I was able to walk away from the after steering table as the weight began to tell on the wire. In fact I had just reached the after end of the boat deck that overlooked the towing wire on the hook when the last restraining seizing went, and the wire shot over the stern like a line, uncoiling itself as when firing a rocket life saving line.

Slowly we drew ahead, and then the weight came on the tow and we were under way; as we drew clear of the channel leading round to the Lohore Straits, the *Griper* came in to pick up her tow on port bow, then she came slowly ahead to draw level with us as we moved westward into the Malacca Straits. The *Takao,* whose once-graceful lines dominated that part of the world, followed pathetically behind us as we drew nearer to her last resting place.

I forgot to mention that the day before leaving Seleter on this particular job, a Lieutenant joined us; he was Peter Embleton RNR, one of the rescue tug skippers who was awaiting passage home from Singapore, and whom the SORT Singapore had asked to help us out with the watch-keeping whilst engaged in towing the *Takao.* He insisted that as I was the mate and he was only there for the ride, he would under take the second mates duties, and would keep the middle and afternoon watches. It turned out that Peter was a near neighbour of mine and hailed from Barkingside, Essex, where I had recently moved to before leaving the UK on my marriage.

Sometime in the evening, whilst towing through the Malacca Straits, the three of us were up on the bridge having a natter when suddenly a light appeared on our port bow, some hundred yards ahead of us. It was a large sailing junk with no other lights and was heading between the two tugs, and in danger of being collected by the towing ropes. We did a hard turn to port, just clearing the surprised crew of the junk by a few feet; they must have wondered what on earth was happening as they crowded her bulwarks to see what was going on. This was something that we had to keep a sharp look out for, as many of the junks were unlit. I had a little difference of opinion with my skipper, who would insist on showing the after steaming light when we had the towing lights illuminated at night.

I could not agree but had to obey orders; though when Peter commented on it later, there was no insistence that it should be kept alight. The next day we reached our destination, and the *Griper* slipped her tow and we steadily pulled the *Takao* her final mile. In the meantime, we were joined by HMS *Newfoundland*, who it would appear was to administer the coup-de-grace after demolition charges had been placed and exploded. The tow was slipped and came straight up and down on our port quarter, where we manoeuvred the wire into the Molly Gogger, which was raised beneath the wire to act as a roller fairlead. Then stopping the wire off whilst the few short turns were passed onto the after capstan, aided by a six inch rope to take

From *Assiduous* before
connecting tow.
Peter Embleton, Lt RNR
(with pipe) and Lt Knight
RNR.

the weight of the rope on the capstan we began the laborious task of
recovering our wire. Oh for the joys of a towing winch, as supplied to
the lease lend tugs and the Bustler and Growler class.

With the rope recovered, we were bidden to make all speed to get
to the other side of the *Newfoundland* so that she could commence
operations; meanwhile a small MFV drew alongside the *Takao* to
take off her remaining crew, and then after some ten minutes drew
slowly away.

The afternoon was still; the sea was like glass with a greasy-
looking surface in the slowly sinking sunlight when a couple of small
explosions could be heard across the intervening distance. Then the
guns of the *Newfoundland* belched into action as the guns teams
were given practice, and with slowness that was almost undectable
at first, the *Takao* began to settle slowly in the water. Gradually
her stern began to disappear, and then her bows lifted as though

she was struggling to remain on the surface; a few moments more, and she slipped beneath the waves, no longer a threat or menace to human life.

We returned to Singapore and the Seleter Harbour a few days later; the commodore paid his long overdue inspection of ship and crew, and congratulations were given all round. The SORT came over afterward, and said 'Oh by the way, we are paying off the *Assiduous* so I want you to go to Columbo to join the *Freedom* that is on refit there, and due to come back into service next month. You will of course be confirmed in your rank as chief officer'. By this time I had been away from home for some eighteen months, and was some six months over my age and service release, my married life was interrupted before I had even had a chance to enjoy being married, so as politely as I could, I told him what to do with his offer, and asked to be sent home at the earliest possible date.

Within a week or so I was on my way, on board the *Brittanic*, the old White Star Liner whose sister ship was the *Georgie,* both of some 27,000 tons; alas the *Georgie* was burned out and became a total loss. I was lucky to be going home with Peter Embleton, who was the senior officer in charge of the Naval Party on board, she being a trooper with some twelve hundred soldiers on board, all homeward bound. I shared the duty of the Duty Naval Officer each day until we reached the UK, some four weeks later. It was not an onerous task, and it worked in our favour when we reached Liverpool some seven days before Christmas 1946, when three drafts had to be escorted to Chatham, Plymouth and Devon port and three other Sub-Lieutenants did the honours whilst Peter and I made our way directly home, to report to Harwich after New Year's Day 1947.

Our trip home was not without drama; an RAF Sergeant who had come on board with a medical escort in Bombay jumped overboard in the Red Sea, and was not recovered even though the ship stopped and lowered away a boat to search the area. Then an emergency operation required the ship to be stopped for an hour during rough weather in the Mediterranean whilst an operation to relieve peritonitis was successfully dealt with.

I was paid off in Harwich with three months foreign service and resettlement leave that took me to April 1947, when once again I was

Crew after inspection.

Officers after inspection. Skipper Bob Slater is at the front, with Jack Gaster looking over his shoulder.

a civilian and resumed my trade as a lighterman, and was once more employed by Messers, William Cory in the lift boat at Purfleet. It was then that I learned from Joe Hardy that his son Bill Hardy, who I had last seen back in 1943 dressed in his RAF uniform of Sergeant Pilot, then flying Mosquito aircraft, had been posted missing presumed killed. My wife's father, who I met so very briefly in October 1943 when he was a Flight Sergeant Engineer in Lancaster Bombers, attached to a Pathfinder Squadron, was posted missing when his plane was shot down on 28 January 1944; it was to be his last flight of his tour of operations.

My wife and I visited his grave in the Reichwald Forest Cemetery many years later. It was poignant to see that he was buried with his fellow crew members, all headstones touching. He, being the eldest at forty years old, was on the left of the row.

I have visited Normandy on four occasions now: in 1984, and again in 1994 for the fortieth and fiftieth anniversaries of D-Day, then in 2004, and again in 2009, and should I still be capable, I will be there with a few more of my old comrades for the Seventieth to honour those men who gave their young lives so many years ago.

In many ways, my last visit in 2009 was the best; I was unable to go in June due to my health, so went in September. It was the first time I was actually able to walk along that sandy beach, and strangely found that I had the energy to walk along it, unaided, without a stick.

I will return to these visits later.

CHAPTER THIRTEEN

# AFTER THE WAR YEARS, RETURNING TO THE THAMES

To restart telling this story after several years have passed is something I find a little daunting; however I shall do my best to follow my return to my beloved Thames. The previous chapters were written more than ten years ago, so now I'm looking even further back than I was to begin with.

I stayed with Cory's for almost a year after leaving the Navy, working the lower reaches of the river from Mucking up to Erith, including Dartford Creek on a regular basis. We were kept busy, taking craft to and from the barge roads to load at Purfleet jetty from the never-ending stream of colliers that unloaded there. That was until I met one old friend who was working for John Hawkins, the Company that had employed me when I first began my apprenticeship.

I had no difficulty in my application to start working with them once more; I found that I was welcomed as though I had never been away, and I enjoyed meeting with some of my old friends. Among them were my old friend George Doman, and another person who had spent his service in the RAF, Harry Farino, together with Alf Carter who, like myself, had been in the Navy. We were glad to be back, and found that working together was just like old times.

George was back on the tug *John Hawkins* – it was a bit bigger than the *Chicken*, the tug he was skipper of before the war. That tug now belonged to Fisher's, another company who worked in the timber trade, and was based in the Surrey Docks. I found myself skipper of the smaller dock tug *The Awk*. It used to be called *The Hawk* until they had to change the name for some reason or other; any way no one on board used their aitches.

The work which we carried out with that tug was very hard, and the hours were long. There was a 6.00 a.m. start every morning which begun at the Canal Lock in the Greenland Dock. This was where we had a berth, where we used to tie up when we had finished the day's graft. We would start by moving all the light barges that we had brought down the canal the previous evening, then form them up in the tow and move on to Canada Dock, and maybe to the New Dock if there were any ships there, and then onward to the Albion Dock, where we would leave the remaining craft. Then we would go around the Surrey Basin into the Stave Dock to get to the Lavender Dock, then by way of the Russia Dock back into Greenland Dock to gather more barges.

After that, we would look around for any craft that were loaded and were to be undocked into the river and place them by the lock, so that could be ready when the lock was manned.

When we were satisfied that craft were where they should be, we retired to 'Lunns', a nice coffee shop where we had our breakfast before starting the rounds again, picking up loaded craft to tow once again to the canal or the Greenland Lock for their onward journey to the place whcre they may be unloaded, be it on the canal or one of the river wharfs.

We would then put a call in to the office, or meet the foreman, who would give the orders to take the loaded craft to wherever they were required. That is to say, wherever they had passes from the customs for the Greenland Lock, or for any of the countless wharves on the riverside, or the Canal Lock for one of the wharves along the canal that ran all the way to Camberwell, or via the Peckham arm to that destination.

We could leave the craft to be put through the Canal Lock by the apprentices, who would make them up in to the tow so that they could be dropped off when their destination had been reached. The hand would secure the barge for offloading, and get the light craft ready to bring down the canal on our return trip.

Meanwhile, we would continue up the canal until our final destination was reached. Then we reversed the tow by picking up the light craft and making our way back to the Canal Basin ready for the morning.

That was what we did for the next couple of years, give or take the winter time when the Baltic iced up and the only timber ships came from Canada, and the work eased off for a few months. Then I was called up to the office, where I was asked if I would take a new tug being built by J. Cooks of Wivenhoe. It was to be called *Thaw*; it was owned by a consortium of business people by the names of Talbot Hawkins and Wells, which gave the tug its name.

The tug was to run as a seeking tug, that is we took any craft that required to be towed from the firms that operated on the river as well the craft owned by John Hawkins. I was informed that my new mate was to be Jack Gatehouse, a man who had lots of experience and was the same age as my father. I was a little bit puzzled by this, but I guess that bosses and their reasons, and as long as we got on together I had no complaints.

It took a little time for me to get used working with Jack, as he always wanted to reverse our roles, but in the end we finally got on the right track and I did get some satisfaction from that.

We had some wonderful tows from the upper reaches, down as far as Benfleet Creek. This was with some rafted timber under the command of Bill Cheal, who regularly did the rafting in the Surrey Docks. The rafted timber was usually taken to where piling was being carried out, either for making new piers or replacing old ones.

We still carried on the work for John Hawkins, either working up Bow Creek with craft for Bow, or for Briant & May, the match factory on the River Lea. These craft carried match sticks all ready to be dipped and boxed up for distributing to the public. We also did a similar job for the Masters Match factory at Barking.

Another job that we had to do was the towing of some craft for W. Michells, who were re-located at the Woolwich Arsenal and did a lot of work for the Ministry of Defence. We managed to get a permanent berth inside the lower end of the 'T pier' at the Woolwich Arsenal, where my father was still working; in fact he often came to a little work shop that was on the end of pier where we berthed. We therefore we had a nice comfortable place, and were well within the travelling distance from home; I was still living in Barkingside at time.

My daughter Anne was born in 1950 at the Ilford Maternity Hospital, but as we did not have a radio on board I was forced to use a public telephone as soon as I got ashore to get on my way home. I was well adrift when I eventually arrived to visit wife and daughter, and the other visitor were on their way out. However, after a quick discussion with the matron, I was able to visit my wife and newly arrived offspring, and what is more I had a late pass whenever I went for a visit until my family came home.

I was still working long hours until each Sunday came around; Saturday was paid up until five, but it was the accepted thing to finish as soon as the work was completed after mid day. I always looked forward to Sundays, when I could relax and take it easy, but there was one Sunday that would change life for a lot of us who worked on the river.

It all began on the Saturday round about 12.00 p.m. I had just taken a barge into Rainham creek, and was on my way back my berth at Woolwich Arsenal when I noticed that water was lapping the top of the river walls. I thought little of it, as the ebb tide had already set in and I was looking forward to a nice few hours at home, so I dismissed it from my mind. On that night, 31 January 1953, the tide had risen so much that Canvey Island and a lot of other low lying places were inundated with rising water, and many peoples' lives were lost.

At 8.00 a.m. on the Sunday morning the telephone rang; we had only just managed to get it installed. It was my boss, Mr. Keith Campbell, who wanted me to go in that morning. He was concerned that some loaded barges were on the tow path on the River Lea, and he wanted me to make my way up Bow Creek with the *Thaw*, enter the lock at Bromley, and proceed up the Lea and pull them back into deep water.

As the *Thaw* was a low-built tug there was no problem getting into position, but I had to wait for the tide to make up that level before I could do anything. The time came when we had sufficient water, and I managed to get them back off the tow-path. All I could do for now was to wait until the water had dropped to the level where we had room beneath the bridges that allow us to regain entrance to Bow Creek, and to make our way to our berth.

That was the beginning of work that went for the next month, where we were employed on making repairs to the river walls by placing old barges in the breaches that the abnormal tide had caused to the wall; we also ferried work people and materials to parts where it was difficult to reach by road.

At this time the work on the Thames was undergoing changes that meant there was going to be a big difference in the way that the timber was shipped, and the way the dockers offloaded and stacked the barges that carried it away to the many wharfs on the Thames. This was the beginning of pre-packaged timber being imported which, in time, meant all one had to do was use a forklift to move and to stow the timber.

There were several wharves that adapted to this type of cargo handling, meaning that the inner London docks lost their work and other places began to pick up it up. This was the start of the elimination of the dock system as we knew it, the beginning of a new era for ports that did not rely on using the Thames, like Felixstowe and a few others.

I then decided to look around for some other form of work that I could do that would give me satisfaction. Then one day a police boat pulled alongside whilst I moored at Greenwich Pier. I got talking to them, and I said that I probably would not get in to the river police, having worked on the river; at least that is what I was told when I went into Wapping Police Station when I came out of the Navy.

They told me that was all nonsense, and they quoted some of the Freemen who were in Thames Division. I decided that I would make an application straight away, as I was thirty years of age and felt that I needed to make sure that I was not too old to apply.

I need not have worried; I passed the entrance exam with flying colours, and after a few months I found myself at Hendon Police College. I had to do at least two years ashore for my probationary period, so I served at Barking on K Division. I found that the pay left me short in the pocket for the first two years after earning the salary of a Tug skipper, though with a few hard years we managed to get through and reaped the benefits later on.

I got through the probationary period okay without too many mishaps; I was in an area that I knew well, and I had met a lot of my old friends from the river who lived in or worked around that area of Barking and Dagenham, adjacent to the Thames. I had a few visits to Court with a few miscreants, but nothing contentious.

Having put my application in for a transfer to Thames Division, I made the most of my time doing duty at my favourite football ground, Upton Park, helping West Ham United; on those few occasions I was in my element. Then the day came for me take the boat test at Wapping Police Station, Thames Division, and pass the interview that followed. I felt that I was back once more on the River that I loved; needless to say I passed, and was soon back on the Thames serving at Blackwall Station.

The clothing that I was issued with bore little resemblance to the Police uniform I had previously worn, and I was less than pleased when I attended Stratford Magistrate Court a few weeks after joining Thames Division, for a case where I was the officer dealing. I was called forward and made my way to the witness box, only to be informed I was using the wrong box. Obligingly I made my way into the other box, and was looking for the Bible to make my affirmation when the Clerk of the Court asked me whether I was the accused. I said no and that I was the officer in the case. I was quickly transferred back to the witness box where I gave my evidence, and the Magistrate, having dealt with the accused, asked if I had left the force to which I replied no, I had joined another Division, and was now in Thames Division.

I should explain that, instead of the normal police officer uniform with silver buttons, in the Thames Division we had a reefer type jacket with black buttons, and the lapels had Thames in silver together with the Number of the Constable thereon, which in my case was 105.

I had a son as well as my daughter Anne; his name is David, and he developed into a boy who seemed to have no fear of anything – especially heights. We were now living in a block of police flats in Vicarage Lane, Stratford, on the second floor above a basement area, with a coal bunker outside of the front door, cantilevered over that drop. It was there that my wife found David sitting, quite happy, until Phyllis said there was something on the television that he would want to see. Thank goodness the ruse worked as he had a thirty foot drop below him..

The first duty I had when I went to Blackwall Station was to be assistant waterside officer; this was a role for anyone who had just joined Thames Division. The idea was to give the new recruits the chance to make their acquaintance with the duty boats, and get

Police launch at the Erith causeway *c.* 1970, (Jack is on the left).

the feel of them when manoeuvring them alongside the pier when coming in to moor up. That is when I made my first acquaintance with Norman Parfitt, the waterside officer that day. He got into the boat moored on the inside of the Pier with, me and showed me what was necessary before getting under way.

He took me through the procedure of checking the oil, fuel and also the water for keeping the engine cool while at the pier; this had to be achieved by making a stern fetch into the inside of the pier. With the tide running this can be quite a difficult manoeuvre: most people joining Thames Division need to be trained to achieve it. He then asked me to do it once more, and I did without any problem. At this he said, 'you have done before haven't you?', and when I told him that I was skipper of small tug before I joined the Police Force he replied, 'You bastard you enjoyed that'. After that we became firm friends.

I stayed at Blackwall for about a year and enjoyed the work that came my way; there were quite a number of barges around at that time, both laden and empty, and among them were a number of loaded craft with cargos of metals, including some of copper, zinc and lead. Also there were a few sugar barges, and at that time they were worth a small fortune. So all in all, that was a lot of valuable items to watch. Then one day I was talking to one of the crew of the Erith duty boat, who said that he was interested in swapping with someone from Blackwall with police accommodation; he had a police house in Erith that was in an ordinary street. I was interested, and after a talk to my wife we started to negotiate for the swap.

We eventually moved into number 28 Church Road, Erith. It was a police house where, at one time, a Police Sergeant lived. It was in a quiet area, and was in a mid-terrace location of a block of houses built in the late Victorian or early Edwardian age. It had a small front garden and a fairly long back garden, which ended with a back gate onto a service alleyway that ran the length of the street. It was a comfortable home that was only a mile from the Thames police station, linked to the conventional station alongside the river towards the rear of the yard.

I settled in quite well on my relief, and was surprised to learn that one of my colleagues was an ex-T124T service man, and what is more

Group photo at rear of Erith Police station, Jack seated second from left.

he was serving on *Assiduous* up until the time I went to join her as mate. In fact he left her on the day that I joined, which proves what a small world it really is; his name was Bob Button.

He had been on the *Assiduous* when she was taken over from Watkins in Plymouth, and had lots to tell me of her previous history. What is more, he could tell where the previous second mate was; he was working next door at Stones Lighterage; his name was Tommy King. There was another person who had been in the tug service by the name of Frank Dott; he was a quarter master on the *Enigma* when I first joined the vessel, but left to become a boatswain on another tug. He was finally made up to second mate, and was commissioned as Sub-Lieutenant T124T. He was working as a waterman for himself, berthing ships when they came into the river.

I found that the working parts of the river were those that I was well acquainted with: to the north, just at the lower end of the Purfleet Rifle Range, and working up from there to the Woolwich Arsenal Canal Entrance on the south bank and the King George Dock Entrance. This took in Rainham and Barking Creeks. The river at that time was still fairly busy, with a lot of smaller ships that could easily go alongside of the numerous jetties of the river wharfs.

In fact there was a pier at Rainham that was built using the remains of the Mulberry harbour, with the spuds anchoring the floating sections as they did in Arromanches. The floating roadway linking to the shore comprised four sections in all, and could berth two ships alongside, and the timber that they carried was carted ashore by trailers.

I found myself in the whaler crew for Erith, and enjoyed every minute of the rowing for the team consisting Bob Button, Bill Armstrong, and several others whose names I can't remember. We rowed in the inter station race, which included Waterloo, Wapping, Blackwall and Erith. It was my first rowing race, and lo and behold we won by two lengths; I was hooked. We went on from there and entered the Gravesend Regetta, rowing Watermans Boats against teams from Essex and Kent River Police crews, which I enjoyed winning; I still have the dishes that we won from that race. We also had races against the Fire Brigade and Navy cadets.

After a lot of time spent studying, I managed to pass the exams for promotion to become a Sergeant, but it was a long wait before we were eligible for promotion; someone said it was like 'waiting for

Sergeant Jack Gaster on older Police launch, with newer version alongside, at Blackwell Police station.

dead men's shoes'. However, that did not stop the service from using you as acting Sergeant, which was unpaid unless you did more than seven days in the rank, but they always found a Sergeant who had to be sent down from Blackwall to prevent that. Anyway, after about two years I found myself newly promoted and sent to Wapping; my new number was Thames 41.

At this point we had moved from the house in Erith, and were occupying a newly purchased semi-detached house in Welling; it was

the start of a lot of hard work for my wife Phyllis and I, in a long
hard slog of decoration and working together to make a comfortable
home for ourselves and our family. Just over two years after that we
had moved into a five bedroom house in Barnehurst. To say it needed
decorating was well and truly a joke, but we got it at a very reasonable
price and never stopped working on it for nearly two years; we
finished up with a four bedroom palace that we occupied until I was
seventy and we moved up to Scotland to our present home.

However, we are rushing it a bit; there is more to say before we get
to that stage. My life changed quite a bit when I went up Wapping;
the main difference was having to start out an hour early every shift,
and at least another hour spent before I arrived home at the end of
the day. The job had changed a bit, and sometimes I had to spend the
first four hours as Station Officer, and then four hours on patrol. Still,
that was part of the job and I soon got used to it. There were times
when I was in the late boat; this occurred when acting as a covering
boat whilst the supervision boat was changing over.

I had no other problems, and soon settled down to whatever came
my way; I soon made friends with all the people that I worked with
including the Inspectors in charge of the reliefs. In due course I was
accepted and settled in to a lively routine.

The Superintendent was someone that I knew, having been the
Inspector of my relief when I first came to Thames Division. So I was
not surprised when he came to me with a request to see if I would
be willing to take on the school talks before the summer holidays,
as there had been a couple of fatal accidents where children had
drowned in the Thames.

I had to get a list of schools near to the river where it attracted
young people; I think he must have known what I got up to when I
was a kid. I readily agreed and, a month prior to the summer holidays,
I began the work and I must say that I enjoyed every talk that I gave,
whether it was for Infants or for Seniors in the fifty or so Schools that
I covered.

I did that job for about three years and found it very rewarding,
and was delighted to be able to congratulate one young lad for
rescuing another boy who fallen into the River Lea by using his jacket
as a way of reaching out to young lad without going into the water
himself, something I had always preached.

Another job I found myself taking charge of was a dragging unit; for instance we went to Hyde Park, searching for some person who was reported to be in the lake. we did not find him in the three days that we were there, but we recovered more than fifty folding chairs for the park authority. I did also get involved as a training officer for a group of new Sergeants who were coming to the Division and had no previous experience, and one Kent Constabulary Sergeant for the Gravesend River Section.

I really enjoyed this work, and after a three week stint they all passed their boat test. The Sergeant from the Kent boat had me to contend with during the next fortnight, as I was seconded to the Kent Boat. It was a pleasure working with the crew for that couple of weeks, and I was sad to leave them.

I did a couple of weeks in the Chief Superintendent's launch whilst the coxswain was on leave. It was so different from the normal working week; I had to slow down once or twice because of the swells that were generated at high speed. I had the feel of being in charge of something that I enjoyed working with, and I felt good, but I was only doing it while the Sergeant who normally did the job was on leave, though it left me feeling very envious of him.

There was one job that came up at a wharf next to our boat yard and near the Town of Ramsgate, a riverside pub with a causeway close by, where the upper torso of a woman was found in the river, causing quite a stir at Wapping on that particular Sunday. During the next few weeks, several pieces of the body turned up in locations as far as several miles downriver near Silvertown, in Woolwich Reach. Unfortunately we failed to recover the head or the hands, and at that time there was no way we could find the identity of the woman, even though we had some of the best CID officers in attendance at Wapping. Most of the body parts were wrapped in newspapers and they appeared to have been in a fridge before being dumped in the Thames.

I eventually returned to Erith when there was a vacancy created by one of their Sergeants retiring, so I was back on what I regarded as the best part of the river, which I had got to know like the backs of my hands. At this time I began to notice how clean the river was becoming, and that I put down to the fact that the dredge mud that used to be taken down to the estuary was being pumped ashore at Rainham Marshes to reclaim some of the low lying lands. This stopped the sludge from returning on the flood tide that used to accumulate on the steps of the station at Erith after every low water, and I presume from the other areas of the river beds.

This was the start of seeing the fish and the bird life returning to the river; from that time on, things began to improve noticeably. There were Cormorants sitting on every buoy that was vacant, either swallowing a large fish or drying wings whilst waiting for the next morsel to appear from the river. This was about 1975, and I had the luck to purchase a twenty one foot cabin cruiser called *Sundowner* for the family and myself.

The *Sundowner* was about five years old, and had a petrol driven motor linked to a stern drive. It was of timber construction with a cascover sheathing. It was lying in a boat yard at the Heybridge Basin near Maldon in Essex when I went to see it, and the owner of the boat yard promised to have it in the water the following weekend. I left to plan the course and to get the necessary stores for the trip back to Erith, and so, armed with a chart of the estuary, my son drove myself and my son-in-law down to collect it.

I went down to the boat on the Friday evening, together with the small dinghy deeply laden with fuel and stores that we would need to do the journey round to Erith. Bob (my son-in-law) and I pulled the dinghy out to the boat over the mud, which was about six inches or so deep. David went off with my car to return home. It was only then that he discovered the oars were still on the roof rack, fortunately we did not have use for them until we arrived home.

We started up the engine as soon as we had enough water around the boat, but just as I decided to get under way I heard the sound of water running from the engine. Someone had drained the engine and forgotten to inform us! Anyway, we looked around for the stopper to seal the water jacket so that we could start the engine once more, but to no avail. It was left to us to find a suitable piece of wood that nearly fit the hole and whittle it down. Then, by using a bit of cloth and hammering it gently, we made it fit. We managed to get under way having lost a few hours and the possible route over the Buxsey sandbank, adding a few hours more to the journey for the homecoming.

During the following few years we had a wonderful time with the *Sundowner*; we found a permanent mooring at Yalding on the

Medway, where the whole family, and many friends, enjoyed the river at one time or other. I very much regretted selling it some five years afterwards when I worked for the Thames Water Authority, but that is another story.

Towards the end of my service with Thames Division I was approached by the Chief Superintendent, who asked me if I would like the job of being his coxswain on the larger Superintendent's launch, based at Wapping. I jumped at the chance, and on the following Monday I reported at Wapping for my orders. I was taken aback when I was told to go to Westminster Pier at 2.00 p.m. to pick up the Prime Minister, Jim Callaghan, and his wife and two grandchildren for a trip downriver, ending up at Wapping for a tour of the Station and the new Workshop.

I did the job for about four months, and was extremely pleased with driving the launch, when I got news that the Thames Water Authority required someone to man a new boat they were getting. I took time to go and see Capt. Cutler, their supervisor, and he appeared to be satisfied with my records of service in the Rescue Tug, and the fact that I was a Freeman with a Waterman and Lighterman's Licences.

He himself was a Lieutenant Commander of Motor Torpedo Boats during the war, working out of Felixstowe, so we had a lot in common that we could talk about. After a while he said he would have liked me to start right away, but I explained to him that I would need to give a months' notice, which he reluctantly accepted. I next went to see the Chief Superintendent to ask if I could expect to stay on for any length of time; his reply was that he could only keep me on until I was fifty-five, only giving me another year, so I told him that if I left now I had the chance of a job with the Thames Water Authority, to which he replied, 'Go get it' and gave me his best wishes.

And so I left the Thames Division a month later. I was soon very disappointed to learn that I could not pick up my Police pension because I had not completed twenty-five years service. I was one year short; my pension was not available until after I reached sixty years of age.

# CHAPTER FOURTEEN

# THAMES WATER AUTHORITY

At the end of November 1977, I left Thames Division and joined the Thames Water Authority as a Coxswain, although until I got the boat that was being built at Cowes on the Isle of Wight sometime in the following July, I was assistant to the Coxswain of the *Thameswater*, skippered by a John Smith, who I previously met whilst I was in Thames Division when I gave him a tow from Blackfriars to Greenwhich pier, as he had a fouled screw a few years earlier.

We got on well together, and I learned a lot from him about the work they were doing, especially the 'river runs' they carried out each week. They started out from Mucking and ended at Teddington on a flood tide, and they ended at Richmond on an ebb tide. It was usually on Wednesday, and it took some ten hours to complete. We carried a chemist from the pollution control section of a sewage treatment plant at Crossness who would analyse the samples of water taken from beneath the boat at given places along the tideway. This was used to produce a graph of the amount of oxygen that was in the river on that day. We also had to take samples, which we put into boxes suitably insulated for the laboratory to sample.

Then we carried out fishing at certain points, beginning at Chapman Sands and working our way upriver to a point just below Barking Creek. This was carried out at the bottom of the tide with the aid of the biologists, who were four in number, led by Mike Andrews, the senior man. We carried out about two or three trawls at each

A moment's relaxation aboard the *Thameswater*, Jack with John Smith.

location, with the depth for each trawl being about one and a half to two metres. Then we moved on to Mucking for our next trawl. We got a variety of small fish and quite a few shrimps, which found their way into our pot that was conveniently full of boiling water.

Thus we progressed upriver, making trawls at Tilbury, Purfleet, and Rainham, until we reached Barking where we usually had just a few fish that could survive the output from the two sewerage plants at Crossness and Beckton, although the river was a lot cleaner than it been for a long time.

Then there was a run that covered the estuary from the Mid-Blythe, where the ships from the Thames Water fleet used to discharge their loads of activated sludge, back to Crossness, taking samples every three miles or so on the way. These samples were taken using a plastic bucket so that there was no metallic evidence for the lab to mark their results. This way of doing the samples proved to be hard work, especially on a windy day when the sea was a bit on the rough side. I used to feel sorry for the chemists when they were sea-sick.

There was another boat owned by the authority named the *Barbel*. It was manned by Arthur Langford, with Eric Humphreys as the assistant coxswain. It was a single screw boat of some forty feet in length. Between us we carried out the duties of attendance of the ships during the change-over of the crews on a Friday each week; this also included changing the laundry bags of each ship, each carrying the bedding for that comprised the fleet. Some of the men came from Beckton who were joining a ship at Crossness, and some arrived at Crossness to be transported to Beckton to join their ship.

There was, of course, the sampling of the waters around the outfalls of the treated sewage discharges of both sites at the low and high water each day. This meant there was a lot of overtime to be had, so each boat would be the duty vessel every other day. Then we delivered the newspapers to be collected from Abbey Wood and taken out to each ship. I did not get down to the *Sundowner* on the Medway too often, and I reluctantly sold it about another year later. However I did hire another boat on the Firth of Clyde during my holidays the following year.

About three months after I joined the *Thameswater*, we had the chance of going to Wimbourn to the Sabre Engine plant, where they built our engines using Ford tractor engines of about eighty horse power, which they stripped down to the bare shell before building it up with new shells and cylinders, pumps, and injectors until they produced a Sabre Marine Diesel engine rated at one hundred and eighty brake horse power.

These were the same engines that were supplied to the boat yard at Wapping for the new fleet of boats that the Thames Division use now. We were lucky to have one of the engineers from Wapping who I knew well, and he stayed in the same bed and breakfast as the wife and I during the week that we were there. I went down the week after John and I had the running of the *Thameswater*; I had Eric Humphreys as my assistant coxswain during that week and we got on very well together.

About three months after I had joined *Thameswater*, we went for the first refit and paint up; we always used two-pot polyurethane, as it stood up to the weather and the constant scrubbing that we did to keep the boat in pristine condition. This was due to the number of distinguished passengers who were interested in the work that we carried out; also there was a lot of time taken up by television programmes that were based on our work. The work was carried out at a small boat yard at Whitstable that was on the sea front, and necessitated putting the boat in a cradle and hauling her up over the beach until we reached the boathouse.

I enjoyed the experience; it made a change from anything that I had done before, though it proved a little bit awkward. When I was putting a few pieces of timber under the cradle to make it smoother when it was pulled over the shingle, I attempted to get a another piece that was sticking out of the beach. I found that it was twenty foot long and was well bedded in; I thought that I had broken my back, which remained sore for a good few days.

The next time we worked with the biologists we had to get a few mussels from the legs of the sea forts that had been built to protect the estuary during the last war. These were an ideal location from where we could harvest a good catch, and there were plenty of the Forts to get round. We took a few samples from each location so that we could get a good specimen of the type of nutriment on which they survived.

About this time the marine superintendent thought that it would be advisable for John and I to take our boatmans licence for the estuary, as we were always out there either doing sampling for the

Queen Elizabeth bridge nearing completion. Taken from the *Thameswater*.

Lab or working with the biologists. He arranged for us to pop up to Seething Lane to take our tests, which we both passed successfully, making us fully covered on the River Thames, from Teddington to a line joining Clacton Pier to Reculvers, including the River Medway. Then we had to take another test for our radiotelephony certificate VHF only. So now we were ready for all that was required of us.

Unfortunately for me, the newspapers got hold of a story that the Thames Water Authority were having a new boat built so that the governors could swan around at their leisure. This was not what the boat was meant for; it was to enable the laboratory and the biologists to do a better job with a boat far better suited for their requirements. The boat was cancelled, and I was left as an assistant coxswain on the *Thameswater*.

Although at times I did take the *Barbell* on the canal run, which started out on the trip from Brentford up to Hayes, then down the Grand Union Canal until we reached Limehouse and the Regents Canal Dock. This would take about three days, sampling all the way.

There were the odd times when John was on leave that I was in command. But they were too few and far between for my satisfaction;

still, it was better than nothing and I did enjoy the job. This went on for another six or seven years; the only consolation was that we went down to Gosport for one refit. We went to Cowes for another, but that did not prove successful because they had used ordinary white enamelm and we had to go back after we had attended the opening of the Thames Barrier. At least that was a better trip; we had a rough journey the first time, and our radar had packed up because one of the wires came out due to the swells being so steep. Fortunately we had reached the Solent by that time, and found that the radar was working on the shorter signals; needless to say we had to get that fixed before we headed home.

We had many VIP trips during the summer months, with visitors from all over the world. We were so proud of our river by now, as it was clean all the way from the estuary to Teddington. The Thames Bubbler, in which we had played a large part, had done its work and the river had more than a hundred and ten species of fish along its whole length.

The Thames Bubbler was the end product of an idea dreamt up by the biologists, who believed if we could pump oxygen into the water it would enable them to sustain more fish within its limits, so we managed to extract oxygen from the atmosphere, and to be able to pump it in to the river when it was required. It was in use very quickly whenever we had a low-oxygen reading on our river runs, normally due to excessive rainfall that brought an overflow from the storm drains in to the river, and this seemed to happen quite a lot. The Thames Bubbler proved to be quite successful, and so the Thames Water Authority had a special self propelled vessel built to cover the whole of the Tideway.

We occasionally had other jobs that took us away from our usual activities for a few weeks. One such job came from someone's idea of putting a radio-active sample in the sludge of one of our ships, the *Hounslow,* and to discharge it in the normal way, and for us to follow on to his track with a tracking device so that we could find out where the sludge settled.

This entailed us being based on the River Crouch at South Farnbridge, so that we were near to the dumping ground between 'number seven buoy' and 'number nine buoy' of the Barrow Deep. As this meant we had to be in the vicinity at low water when the ship approached, we had to time our arrival so we were out there for every low water come rain or shine; it was a tough time. On the second week that we were there, I had an arrangement with Cliff Jeavons, our new coxswain of the launch *Barbell,* to swap places because my wife Phyllis was far too unwell to leave her for another week. He took over my place, whilst I took the *Barbell* on the regular work of the Thames, which gave me time to look after her. Cliff was a Freeman of the Company of Watermen and Lightermen, so we worked well together.

Some three months after the work in the Estuary, we had to take some samples using a grab to check anywhere showing traces of the radio-active elements that were included in the sludge deposited by the *Hounslow* during the time of the experiment. We had a length of wire, which we streamed out from the stern, with a sensor fitted on the end to give a warning when there were any radio-active impulses, of which there were quite a few, so we made several grabbing operations. But none of the radio-active samples tied up with the samples from the *Hounslow,* meaning these must have came from Sizewell, the only atomic power station in that area. The experiment proved a success; all the sludge had been absorbed by the tidal streams in the estuary.

Another deviation from our regular work came one day when we took out a party of Chinese gentlemen who came to see what we were doing to improve the river; they were from a similar working arrangement to ourselves and were engaged on cleaning up the rivers in their country. We got on very well with them, and asked them if they would care to take lunch with us at Greenwich at the 'Cutty Sark' public house, which they graciously accepted. They had one person in their party who spoke very good English and acted as an interpreter for the rest of the party. We had a good meal which they thoroughly enjoyed, and after the meal they chose me to thank, because I was the eldest.

By now things were happening within the Thames Water Authority; with the demise of the GLC they were now in control of a number of piers, together with the men, of which quite a few were Freemen of the Company of Watermen and Lightermen. Someone thought it would be a very good idea to have us working from Festival Pier, and to come under their command; also they thought we were earning too much money, not thinking of the amount of overtime we incurred doing our job to the best of our ability.

It looked certain that was going to happen, so John and I were offered the chance of being made redundant. I was sixty three at that time, and my wife was suffering from allergies which were making it hard for her to cope. Also we had her mother staying with us who needed care, so both John and I decided to accept redundancy; although John was ten years younger than me, he also decided he had enough. We were given a good send off from the fleet of ships, and a party from the people with whom we had worked for past nine or so years.

I had to sign on at the department of labour in Bexleyheath, and this is where I received a big shock. As I was over the age of sixty I would receive no money, although they expected me to sign on every week. Needless to say, I said that if a job came up that needed someone with my experience I would accept, otherwise I was happy to leave them waiting. I have never had any money that I haven't earned in all of my life, so I would see them in hell before bowing to them.

I kept in touch with Cliff, who had changed his boat and was now in command of the *Melisa*. He was doing the work that we used to do, tending the ships at Crossness and Beckton. The *Thameswater* was now operating from London, but they were already experiencing trouble.

Apparently the people who had the running of the boat, that is the coxswains and the assistants, had no idea of what they were doing; apparently they almost sunk the boat on one occasion, and were finding it difficult to keep running. John and myself had given the people who came to us all the required knowledge that was necessary, but they were relieved by someone with little knowledge of what was necessary, and the boat was laid up for some time.

In the meantime, I was busily engaged in building up the funds of the Royal Naval Commando Association which had just got off the ground; in fact, whilst we had been at Gosport for our annual refit, I had the *Navy News* in which I saw a request, by a person with name of Jungle George, for past members of the Naval Beach Commandos to write to him with the view of forming an association. I contacted him, and we formed a small group of about forty people who spread the news, and by the time we were finished we had almost two hundred people joining.

I took on the job of Treasurer after the first year, and held that position for over four years, but gave it up when my wife's health

*Left:* D-Day veteran Jack Gaster, of J Commando.

*Below:* RN Commando memorial, on the site of the training HQ HMS *Armadillo.*

gave me concern; still, I made quite a bit of money for the funds by giving talks about the River, and our part in the D-Day effort.

I attended the fortieth D-Day anniversary, and the fiftieth when we went on the *Canberra* to the D-Day beaches. Since then I have been twice on the sixtieth and sixty-fifth visits, and I daresay I'll go again while I can make it. There is something that drives me on to say thank you for being alive when so many died on that day.

After six months of missing my old environment, I hired a narrow boat from Kingston with my wife, daughter, son-in-law, and my two youngest grandchildren. We set off to proceed upriver, to places of which I had very little knowledge. We arrived at Windsor and were enjoying ourselves when my wife ate something that started her allergies flaring up, meaning we had to go back to Kingston for our car and return home. Meanwhile my daughter and her family continued to enjoy the rest of the week on board.

When I returned home, there was a message to phone the laboratory to speak to Peter, who was the chief chemist. He asked if I would be interested in working on the *Thameswater*, as he had a problem with the people who were running in now.

Apparently they were a private company who were not experienced with the ways the laboratory worked. He told me that I would have to form a company, and put in writing my terms for dealing with Thames Water Authority. I quickly found out what the other people were charging and based myself on that, having first consulted my son David on what form my Company should take.

Thus TAMERS was born, standing for Thames and Medway Emergency River Services, 'Jack Gaster & Co'. My wife Phyllis and I were Directors, and we put in our tender. It was accepted, so at the age of sixty-four I was in charge of my own destiny. I had a few people that I could call on to act as my assistant, and I paid them a fair wage. I later apprenticed my grandson Jason, who spent two and a half years with me before he fell for a girl up in Scotland and decided that was where his destiny lay.

I started with a run every week on the sampling, and whenever there was a trip for visitors to the river I made myself useful. They seem to have got the taste for it now, and we usually found one trip for visitors every week. Then, of course, there was the odd emergency run that took a couple of days to deal with. A half day for

*Thameswater* at the Thames Barrier, *c.* 1985.

maintenance of the engines, and that completed the week. I was in heaven once more.

We had a sampling run on a weekly basis, with an Estuary run once a month. I had troubles with the port engine, which used to cut out when it got over heated. I soon found out the trouble when I dismantled the cooling pipe; it had been put in the wrong way so that the engine cut out as soon as it reached the required temperature instead of working properly. It was a mistake made by the Marina, who last sorted out the problem when the other people were running the boat.

Whilst Jason was attending classes during his apprenticeship at Gravesend, I invited George Saunders to bring the rest of his class out for estuary run with the *Thameswater*. It was a success and we managed a few trips while I was doing the runs; I think that the lads got quite a kick out of those runs.

Round about that time, I was pleased to meet the only female licensed apprentice, a Miss Sheila McGeown, who had been knocked back on her bid for her Freedom. She came to me for a couple of trips and worked quite well before sitting the tests again, which she passed with flying colours; in fact I employed her several times after that.

During the course of conversation I discovered her Grandmother lived close to me before the war.

I suppose that I met quite a few people who came on board the *Thameswater* during the time I skippered her; a number of them were looking toward the docklands before that building was started. I suppose they were friends of the managers of Thames Water Authority. I had to change the name of the boat when we were taken over by the Environment Authority. The boat's name was changed to the *Thames Guardian;* however I still had the same people in charge – they were taken over at the same time.

I had to change my venues when I wanted any repairs that I could not do, so I made arrangements with the Police workshop, with which I had very good relations. They had a trolley that could take the weight of the *Thames Guardian* and that fitted on their boat lift. So any time I wanted to lift the boat, providing I gave them reasonable notice, they would facilitate me. It worked quite well, except for one occasion when the person in the office of the laboratory demanded the boat be put into the water for a visit by some bigwig. I told them that was beyond their power as the boat was not ready, and I could not take the responsibility of running the boat in that condition. I'm afraid that I had to go higher up before they saw reason. I did not get any come back from that episode.

I attended, with the *Thames Guardian*, the Erith Regatta that year. It was a nice sunny day, and there were several boats from the Navy, Custom and excise, the Port Health, and Police in attendance so we made it a day to remember. There were some my old friends from my days in the River Police who now had their own sailing boats that belonged to the Erith Yacht Club, a very well respected club on the Thames. So I was not alone for long.

We were coming to the end of my time with the *Thames Guardian;* I had now passed the age of seventy, and my wife thought it would be a good time to retire. We had been looking around for another house for some time, and had seen a bungalow for sale up in Scotland whilst we were visiting my daughter who was now settled in there, close to Lochmaben. We had been up to Dunoon for a reunion with our Commando friends at the time when we first saw the property, it was situated on Mill Loch, and it was everything that I hoped for. I could get a small boat and spend a few hours on it if ever I felt the need.

As it turned out the, *Thames Guardian* was to be replaced by another boat that had been put together by a committee, and would not have suited me, so I was glad to have been there whilst we had a boat that looked and felt like something one could be proud of. And so we left behind my time on the Thames, one that I never can or would ever forget. I made many friends throughout my life on the river, some gone but not forgotten, others are still alive and kicking. I miss them all.